THE BIG 10 FISH & SEAFOOD COOKBOOK

Cioppino, page 145

TERRI DIEN

THE BIG 10

FISH & SEAFOOD COOKBOOK

10 SEAFOOD	80 RECIPES	240 VARIATIONS

ROCKRIDGE PRESS

Interior and Cover Designer: Matt Girard

Art Producer: Janice Ackerman

Editor: Carolyn Abate

Production Editor: Chris Gage

Photography: © 2019 Darren Muir. Food Styling by Yolanda Muir.

Vintage Nautical Illustrations: Mr. Vintage/creativemarket.com.

Author Photo: Courtesy of Carolyn Shek.

ISBN: Print 978-1-64152-995-2 | eBook 978-1-64152-996-9

R0

For my family: Alice, Jacob, Tim, Erica, J. R., Emilia, Everly, Alex, Brian, and my husband, Paul. For their love and support and for never complaining about my food.

CONTENTS

Shrimp and Pineapple in Thai Red Curry, page 126

INTRODUCTION

Fish and seafood have been a part of my life for as long as I can remember. Both my parents love seafood, and we ate it as often as possible. "Fish is good for your brain!" they would insist. Fearing that I wouldn't have a healthy brain, I ate as much of it as I could. A tuna fish sandwich on a toasted plain bagel became my favorite snack.

I grew up in lower Manhattan, in the neighborhood of the South Street Seaport near the Fulton Fish Market's original location. Weeknight dinners often included a steamed fish that my mom bought live in Chinatown. In the summer, we enjoyed pans of seafood paella the size of bus hubcaps. When I got sick, I'd get a deep bowl of red clam chowder instead of the traditional chicken noodle soup. We celebrated the New Year with my dad's homemade bouillabaisse. When we moved to San Francisco, I discovered new favorites, specifically California sushi rolls, cioppino, steamed Dungeness crab, and white clam chowder served in a sourdough bread bowl.

In college, I liked to impress friends with my cooking. Linguine with clams was a go-to recipe—at first using canned clams, because a can opener and hot plate were all I had access to in a college dorm room. Once I started living on my own, I graduated to fresh clams. When the George Foreman grill came out, it became my favorite way to grill salmon because it would cook the fish evenly—my first ever life hack.

In culinary school, I learned fish butchery, as well as advanced fish cookery. We learned how to fillet salmon one day; how to skin it the next. I got good and fast at peeling 20 pounds of shrimp. One of my first restaurant jobs was in a seafood restaurant, where I shucked thousands of oysters, made countless sushi rolls, and steamed dozens and dozens of clams and mussels.

For the last 15 years, I've been a chef instructor, teaching people from all walks of life how to cook. Among the classes I enjoy the most are the ones in which we cook fish, make paella, or grill shrimp. Being a chef instructor is so rewarding when we get to discuss the health benefits of eating more fish, what sustainability means, and how to eat more sustainably at home. I know it's confusing to most folks: Is cooking fresh fish always best over frozen fish? When it comes to omega-3 fatty acids and omega-6 fatty acids, it can be confusing to know which one is healthier. It's hard to know if farm-raised fish are good or bad for the environment, especially if you aren't aware of the specific issues—and it was my honor and privilege to bring that information to my students in a manner that was engaging and fun.

My hope is that this book will become an extended lesson for you. In 80 recipes, we will cover the 10 main fish that are not only sustainable and eco-friendly but also healthy and nutritious. I have also included information on different cuisines and cooking techniques, so you'll learn new things in addition to becoming more comfortable cooking with fish. Hopefully, you'll be able to take these as foundational guidelines and create some signature versions of your own.

FISH FOR LIFE

"In the hands of an able cook, fish can become an inexhaustible source of perpetual delight."

—Jean-Anthelme Brillat-Savarin (1755–1826)

I hope this book becomes a source of inspiration as you discover the many ways to enjoy fish and seafood. My aim is to make you a more confident cook and provide you with a supply of go-to recipes so you'll never get tired or bored of eating the same thing.

We'll cover all the benefits of eating fish, including how to buy sustainably and when it is appropriate to use fresh, frozen, and canned. You'll be amazed at how easy it can be to incorporate more fish into your diet without much effort.

WHAT'S GREAT ABOUT FISH

Fish is delicious and is one of the healthiest proteins you can add to your diet. Fish offers a variety of health benefits, including having many essential nutrients and helping with brain function, vision, and sleep.

The most important nutrient of all has to be the omega-3 fatty acids present in fish. Omega-3s are linked to helping lower LDL cholesterol levels, which can improve heart health. If you are pregnant or just recently had a baby, omega-3s are really important in prenatal and postnatal neurological development. Omega-3s can also help reduce inflammation and help slow the development of Alzheimer's disease in older people. Fish is also a great source of vitamin D, which can help with your body's ability to absorb calcium for bone strength.

If you are looking for ways to lower the amount of saturated fats in your diet, consider adding more fish to your plate. As a protein source, fish has significantly less saturated fat than beef or chicken, making it a lean protein that can help reduce the risk of certain cancers and other health problems.

THE TRUTH ABOUT MERCURY

When it comes to eating fish, a key concern is the amount of mercury found in many common types of fish and what it means for our health. Mercury is particularly toxic to a child's developing brain and nervous system. The US Food and Drug Administration warns women who may become pregnant or are pregnant or nursing, babies, and young children to avoid fish with high amounts of mercury.

A general rule of thumb to consider is that fish at the top of the food chain contain higher mercury levels. Take, for example, shark, which contains one of the highest mercury levels found in fish. Tuna also carries a high risk of mercury poisoning if consumed in large quantities. Smaller fish, such as sardines or mackerel, carry the least amount of mercury, as they are at the bottom of the food chain.

According to the National Resource Defense Council, shark has levels of mercury in the 0.979 PPM (parts per million) while salmon, sardines, and tilapia have levels in the range of 0.009 to 0.022 PPM, according to the Food and Drug Administration.

The best and most accessible seafood advisory resource is Seafood Watch, a program developed by the Monterey Bay Aquarium in California. Their information is also available via an app for both iOs and Android platforms.

OOOOH THAT SMELL

In *Poor Richard's Almanac*, Benjamin Franklin famously wrote, "Fish and visitors stink in three days!" I am not sure what types of visitors Ben had, but you can keep fish longer than three days now thanks to modern refrigeration.

Fresh fish should smell like the body of water from which it was caught. Fresh fish from the sea should give off a briny ocean scent. Freshwater fish—such as tilapia, catfish, and trout—do not possess the same amino acids as sea fish; however, they do suffer from a similar odor-indicating breakdown that causes them to smell or taste "muddy" instead.

According to the American Society for Nutrition, that bad smell associated with fish comes from their physiology. Fish use certain amino acids to help balance salt levels in their cells. When the fish are killed, bacteria and enzymes convert the amino acids to another compound that gives off that "fishy" odor.

To reduce fishy odor, rinse the fish in cold water to wash away any surface compounds. Treating the fish with acid—such as lemon, vinegar, or tomato—is another option. Acid makes the compounds bind with water instead of more of the amino acids, and thereby they become less volatile.

Remember, if a piece of fish you are about to consume smells like mud or ammonia, don't eat it. Always practice the philosophy of "when in doubt, throw it out."

THE BEST FISH

There are many fish for you to choose from, and this book will help break down for you the 10 we've selected. We based our selection on availability, price point, sustainability, and, of course, health.

Accessible to Many

When you think about cooking fish, the first thing that comes to mind is perhaps a beautifully displayed fish counter with heaps of ice and beds of fresh kelp. Or maybe a large assortment of frozen fish.

Whatever you envision, the recipes in this book can bring more variety to your table, regardless of the types of fish that are available to you. We will offer plenty of substitutions so you can adjust recipes based on what is available in your area—fresh, frozen, or canned. Go with what's appropriate and available and you'll never make the wrong choice.

Cost Conscious

Buying fresh fish can be expensive, especially when you are looking for wild-caught and sustainable choices. However, frozen and canned fish are widely available and shouldn't be overlooked.

Frozen fish is generally more affordable than fresh fish and can be used in many recipes without compromising flavor and texture. In other recipes, canned fish has the starring role, where fresh or frozen can't compete.

The point is, the cost of fish shouldn't be a deterrent to eating more fish. There is an available fish to fit everyone's budget; and with some creativity and know-how, you can transform the most basic, cheapest piece of fish into a fantastically delicious dish.

Good for Your Health

The American Heart Association recommends eating fish at least twice a week—especially fatty fish, such as salmon, mackerel, sardines, trout, and tuna, which are high in omega-3 fatty acids. Eating a diet rich in omega-3s lowers your risk of developing cardiovascular disease. It can also lower your blood pressure and keep harmful plaque from building up in your arteries. What's more, these fatty acids also reduce inflammation in the body, can help curb depression and anxiety, and are great for your skin. Fish is also a great source of protein without any saturated fats.

Eco-Friendly

Even though consumers are encouraged to eat more fish and seafood for health reasons, social awareness over some fishing industry methods that compromise and threaten ocean ecosystems has made it challenging. As consumers, we have a responsibility to be mindful when we make our choices. In the last 20 years, our efforts have paid off, but we can't stop there. We have to keep sustainable seafood a priority.

Sustainable seafood is seafood that is managed and fished using practices that will ensure there will be more to catch in the future. It's making sure seafood farming yields the highest nutritional value as though it were caught in the wild, while at the same time not harming the environment.

Aquaculture, as it is now called, is still working on ways to increase sustainable practices, but now more than ever, consumers have options to make the right choices. Here is the list of fish and seafood we are covering in this book, as well as a brief description of the best choices, alternatives, and what to avoid, with thanks to Seafood Watch.

It's easier now to make good choices when shopping for seafood. The food labeling law passed by Congress in 2004 requires grocery stores to label their seafood for sale under a "country of origin labeling" (or COOL). For seafood products to be labeled with "United States" as the country of origin, they must be derived exclusively from fish or shellfish hatched, raised, and processed in the United States.

SALMON: Wild salmon that has been caught in the Pacific Ocean, particularly in the United States and in Canada, is the best choice. Chinook and coho salmon should be avoided. Any sustainably farm-raised salmon can be an option, as long as it is farmed from Maine, British Columbia, or New Zealand, due to their eco-friendly farming methods.

TUNA: Tuna is a large category to navigate, as it is found all over the world. Tuna that has been caught using handline, hand-operated pole and line, or trolling are all good choices. Types of tuna that are particularly good include albacore (from the Atlantic or Pacific Oceans), skipjack, and yellowfin.

SARDINES: Fresh sardines are high in omega-3s, and because they are so small and grow so quickly, they have very low mercury levels. They are considered to be plentiful at the moment and are also very inexpensive. Canned sardines are also a good choice to consider because many recipes call for them.

MACKEREL: If you haven't tried mackerel before, now is your chance. It happens to be one of the most sustainably caught fish on the market. It's rich flavor and high omega-3s are unmatched even by its more popular cousin, salmon.

TILAPIA: Tilapia is one of the freshwater fish we are covering in this book. Nearly all tilapia is farmed in indoor recirculating tanks. It's always best to choose tilapia from Peru or Ecuador and avoid fish from China.

CATFISH: Catfish is as versatile as chicken, due to its mild flavor. A sustainability success story, nearly all farm-raised catfish come from recirculated fresh indoor pools or ponds in the United States and around the world. Avoid farm-raised catfish from China.

TROUT: Trout farming is the oldest domestic aquaculture industry in North America, beginning in the 1880s in Idaho. Technically, rainbow trout are freshwater cousins of salmon. While rainbow trout are freshwater, steelhead trout are saltwater fish.

SHRIMP: Sustainably farmed and wild-caught shrimp from the United States and Canada are plentiful and versitile. They are prepared in nearly every cuisine and make every dish so tasty and special. Keep a two-pound bag of frozen shrimp in your freezer and you'll always have something delicious to make for dinner.

CRAB: Blue crabs are the most eco-friendly and sustainable crab choice because they mature and reproduce quickly. They are found on the East Coast, particularly from the Chesapeake Bay and along the mid-Atlantic seaboard. Dungeness crab caught in the Pacific Ocean in Oregon waters is the most sustainable choice for this species, according to the Marine Stewardship Council.

CLAMS AND MUSSELS: Clams and mussels, both bivalves in the mollusk family, are considered to be the most eco-friendly and sustainable seafood produced currently. According to food scientists, bivalves are the most ethical choice for aquaculture since they are stationary, don't require feeding, don't need extra space, and filter their own nutrients from the water.

WHAT YOU DON'T SEE HERE

There are 10 chapters in this book, covering 11 different types of fish and seafood with a focus on increasing sustainability. There is bound to be something in here for everyone to enjoy.

But what about the other types of fish that are so popular? Why just these 10? I've been trying to answer these questions myself, knowing that my love for seafood isn't limited to just these 10. Halibut, sea bass, cod, swordfish, and even lobster are delicious and crave-worthy, too. However, the 10 in this book are overall produced and harvested with the most sustainable options. With this book, we encourage you to explore the options available in your own area to make the best choices possible for your community, our planet, your overall health, and of course, your bottom line.

SUSTAINABILITY MATTERS

What's a sustainable choice? It can be made based on conservation of the species of fish, environmental and ecological concerns, health and nutritional concerns, financial constraints, or combinations of all four considerations. The goal is to maintain a certain rate or level of product without depleting fish resources. But it can be overwhelming to make the right buying decision with all these factors to consider.

Say, for example, you want to cook salmon for dinner. Your decision can take you in a number of directions. You might want to go with the farm-raised salmon at the market because it's the cheapest per pound. But the farm-raised salmon actually tends to have less protein and lower amounts of omega-3s, and farm-raising practices can pollute the environment.

So let's look at the wild-caught salmon. Turns out that's out of your price range. Maybe there's another option? What about the farm-raised salmon in the frozen section that has "sustainably farm-raised" on its label? Smart choice—sustainable salmon farms are taking measures to reduce toxic pollution. They use less chemicals and antibiotics and maintain acceptable levels of protein and healthy omega-3s. The price is also consumer friendly, though slightly more expensive than the regular fresh farm-raised salmon you were considering.

Overwhelmed? Yes, but in order for us to keep salmon available to future generations, it's important to think of the consequences of our choices. Tell yourself,

"I'm choosing this fish because . . . ," and fill in the blank. The reasons could be personal preference, nutritional, or ecological. I encourage you to turn to the Seafood Watch app. It will provide you with seafood options based on a host of factors to best suit your needs.

WHAT TO LOOK FOR WHEN BUYING FISH

When shopping for fish, one can get easily overwhelmed by the selection available. The dizzying offerings from the fresh seafood counter, the vast freezer section, the canned fish aisle, and what about wild-caught versus farm-raised? And what about price or sustainability?

Once you have a bit of information under your belt, your next trip to the market will be easier to navigate and you'll have an easier time making the right choice.

For fresh fish:

The eyes should be clear, wet, and shiny. The tail and side fins should be full and intact. It should feel firm, wet, cold, and slippery, but not slimy. Press down and the flesh should spring back. Pass on any fish that feels sticky or soft.

If the fish you're buying has gills, pull back on each side and have a look. They should be clean and red. Run your hands over the scales, they should feel firm and look shiny. Dry, brittle scales indicate old fish.

For frozen fish:

Frozen fish is the most sustainable option. In many situations, it's also less expensive and could be the most appropriate choice.

Fish and seafood are now frozen using a method called flash freezing. It occurs on the boat where the fish are caught or in a processing facility as soon as they are brought in or harvested. This method prevents large ice crystals from forming in the fish's cells, which can compromise the texture of the fish once defrosted and cooked. Flash-frozen fish come in individually vacuum-packed portions, so you can thaw as much as you need and keep the rest frozen.

Oftentimes, some of the "fresh" fish you see on the ice beds at the seafood counter might actually be tagged as "previously frozen." If you have defrosted fish on your hands, do not refreeze it. If you come across frozen fish with lots of ice-crystal buildup in the package or freezer burn, avoid buying it.

For canned or tinned fish:

Canned fish is caught and preserved so that it remains at its best as a shelf-stable product for even longer than frozen fish. Canned fish is ready to eat and comes already packed in oils that can improve the flavor of virtually anything you are preparing.

The fish used for canning are predominantly of the smaller type: sardines, skipjack tuna, and mackerel. Because they are shelf-stable, it doesn't take any refrigeration at all to store the fish and it takes little energy to process them, except that used to package them into the cans. The fish also doesn't spoil until the can is opened, eliminating unnecessary food waste. Canned fish is also the least expensive on the market.

PEAK SEASON

Eating seasonally is not just limited to fruits and vegetables. Fish and shellfish are seasonal, too. We have become accustomed to eating every variety of fish any old time of year and that sacrifices flavor, freshness, and the nourishment of the soul that comes from looking forward to a dish that only comes at certain times of the year.

If you've ever heard of the phrase "Buy seafood only in months with an 'r' in it," it's for good reason. Those months tend to be the cooler months of the year, so waters will be colder and the seafood, if it is to be wild-caught, will have less bacterial activity than it would in warmer temperatures. There is less of a concern for seasonal eating in farm-raised fish, such as tilapia, catfish, and farmed shellfish.

Enjoy crab in the cooler months, from late October through early February. Salmon is abundant between May and October, and trout is in high season from April to November.

Sustainability Labels and Seals

To be labeled for sale as sustainable, seafood has to be harvested in a such a way that other sea life or the ecosystem where the seafood is found isn't harmed in any way. It ensures that all types of seafood can be enjoyed by future generations. There are several organizations that monitor the practice of commercial fishing. When you are at the market, look for labels to indicate certified sustainability.

The Marine Stewardship Council (MSC) is a nonprofit organization founded in London, England, that sets, monitors, and audits the standards for sustainable fishing all over the world using a science-based set of requirements.

The Aquaculture Stewardship Council (ASC) monitors seafood farming, or cultivators of fish and seafood from around the world. They don't certify seafood farms, but they do permit the use of their logo on products that meet their sustainability standards. When you see their logo, it means the fish has been responsibly sourced with minimal impacts on society and the environment and is fully traceable back to a well-managed farm.

Best Aquaculture Practices (BAP) has designed their aquaculture certification program to be compliant with the Global Food Safety Initiative (GFSI), Global Social Compliance Programme (GSCP), and Global Sustainable Seafood Initiative (GSSI).

SMALLER IS BETTER

Size matters, and in this case, smaller is better for the environment. Choosing smaller fish—such as sardines, anchovies, mackerel, and the smaller types of tuna, like skipjack—is a great way to eat fish in a sustainable manner.

These smaller fish are at the lower end of the food chain. They reproduce quickly, are in more abundant supply, contain the lowest amounts of mercury, and aren't as vulnerable to overfishing as larger fish like tuna. Current food trends are moving toward eating more of these smaller fish to give the larger ones an opportunity to replenish their populations. The bonus, actually, is that these smaller fish are quite tasty, high in beneficial nutrients, and low in harmful substances.

MUST-HAVE EQUIPMENT

The idea here isn't to buy specialized tools for fish butchery, but rather to make sure you have the necessary tools and cookware to cook and eat fish. I've put together a short list of must-haves, items that I believe must be in your kitchen for successful home cooking.

CUTTING BOARDS: Your boards should be plastic, wood, bamboo, or composite material and large enough to give you ample space on which to prep your fish and vegetables.

CHEF'S KNIFE: The best chef's knife is one that feels the most comfortable in your hand. A sharp knife is a safe knife, so make sure to get your knives sharpened regularly.

SERRATED KNIFE: The sharp serrated teeth of this knife make your work easier when it comes to slicing baguettes, tomatoes, or flaky pastry crust.

SERRATED VEGETABLE PEELER: The micro-teeth on the peeler's blades cut through vegetable skin much easier and stay sharper longer than the straight-edged variety.

TONGS: One of the few times you'll hear me advise that cheaper is better. Kitchen tongs should be lightweight, about 12 inches in length.

WOODEN SPOONS: A couple of wooden spoons are useful for stirring sauces, stirring batters, and testing fry oil temperatures. Wood doesn't transfer heat as quickly as metal, so it's easier to handle.

FISH-TURNING SPATULA: The spatula's blade is thin and flexible and its sharp edge slides underneath crispy panfried fish easily. You'll find its edge is slightly angled so you can move it around in tight spaces.

SLOTTED SPOON: A metal slotted spoon can help scoop dumplings out of frying oil or lift steamed mussels from their cooking liquid.

FISH TWEEZERS: Perfect for removing the pin bones, the small bones at the ends of nerve endings that radiate out from the spines of fish. They are embedded in the flesh and hard to remove without mangling the fish.

CAST IRON SKILLET: This versatile pan is great for heartier fish and fish that you want to develop a crunchy crust. It has a great ability to retain heat and can go from stovetop to oven.

SEAFOOD CRACKER AND CRAB PICKS: Seafood tool sets that include seafood crackers and picks make it easier to open the shells and extract the delicate meat inside crab legs and claws.

HOW TO REMOVE PIN BONES FROM FISH FILLETS

Before cooking a fish fillet, it's always a good idea to check it for pin bones. The more gourmet markets will sell fillets with bones already removed, but sometimes they miss a few. They can't really be seen, as they sink below the surface of the fillet and run diagonally through the fish's flesh. The best way to check for them is to run your fingers down the length of the fish along the center white line.

Once you have determined they are present and need removal, place the fillet over an inverted bowl. The curve of the bowl helps the bones stick out a bit for easier location and removal.

Firmly grip one end of the bone with fish tweezers or needle-nose pliers and pull very slowly, wiggling it slightly until the bone pulls free. Pull in the direction the bone is pointing, as not to tear the flesh too much. Repeat until all of the pin bones have been removed.

INGREDIENTS THAT BUILD FLAVOR

Building flavor is a crucial part of any cooking process. With fish, it's even more important, because the protein tends to have a delicate flavor. Fats and oils, citrus and acids, and herbs and spices are perfect cooking companions for any fish or shellfish. With the right combination and use of these aromatics, you can show off your cooking skills like a pro.

Fats and Oils

Oils can be used for cooking, marinating, and finishing fish and seafood. Fats add a lot of flavor, not to mention delivering heat to the fish. Some of the best medium- to high-temperature oils and fats include:

- Butter

- Canola oil

- Corn oil

- Grapeseed oil

- Peanut oil

- Pure olive oil (more refined and can be cooked at higher temperatures)

- Rendered bacon fat

- Safflower oil

- Vegetable oil

Citrus and Acid

Another element that can enhance the flavor of fish is citrus, or more broadly, acid. Citrus and fish are a match made in heaven. The juice can neutralize and stop the chemical compounds in fish that give off that fishy smell and taste. Acidic ingredients that pair nicely with fish include:

- Capers and olives: Try adding these to mackerel, salmon, and tuna.

- Lemon juice

- Lime juice

- Mustard: Catfish, tilapia, and mussels go especially well with a small amount of mustard.

- Pomegranate juice
- Vinegar: My favorites are red wine, champagne, sherry, and white balsamic.

Herbs and Spices

The last piece of the aromatic picture is herbs and spices. They are a fantastic way to introduce flavor without adding extra fat or calories. If you taste your dish and feel like it needs something, before reaching for more salt or butter, add some herbs or spices. Try some of these classic combinations:

- Chile powder, cumin, and cilantro: Smoky, spicy, and bright, these spices bring the Southwest to salmon, mackerel, tuna, tilapia, catfish, or shrimp.
- Fennel seeds and tarragon: Give salmon and tuna a hint of the south of France using these two with a splash of white wine or lemon juice.
- Lemon and dill: This classic pairing is as traditional as it gets and for good reason. They complement each other perfectly.
- Lemongrass and ginger: Pair with some lime juice for a Thai-inspired dish on tilapia, catfish, salmon, shrimp, and mussels.
- Parsley and smoked paprika: Try using this combination with shrimp, mussels, salmon, and mackerel.
- Thyme and mustard: Create a distinctly French flavor for fish like salmon and tuna. You can add a splash of white wine or dry vermouth to make it extra special.

FISH FAT AND FLAVOR

Not all fish look and taste the same and therefore are not all perfectly interchangeable. What makes fish compatible for substitutions is their fat content. Fatty fish can substitute for one another without much compromise in taste or mouthfeel.

Fish like mackerel can stand in well for tuna, sardines, and some larger anchovies. Salmon can substitute for mackerel or tuna and, in many cases, shrimp. How fishy the fish tastes can also help you find substitutes.

You can also tell by the texture and color of their flesh. Large, heavy flakes present in the cooked flesh indicate similar textures, and therefore fat content. If the flesh is finely flaky, like catfish, tilapia, and trout, the fish has low levels of fat and would make good substitutes for one another.

ABOUT THESE RECIPES

I'm so fortunate to have this opportunity to offer the recipes in this book to you. There are 80 recipes for cooking fish and seafood, as well as nearly 240 variations total, about two for each recipe. Many of these are favorites that I am excited to share with you. I've tried to include a good variety that are simple, as well as some that might be a challenge, if you are up for the task. There are recipes perfect for a quick weeknight dinner and some that would be perfect for a special occasion or dinner party.

For each recipe, I've specified the type of fish you should use and when it would be appropriate to use canned, frozen, or fresh. For instance, fresh clams would be awesome in a recipe for linguine and clams, but if fresh clams aren't available, frozen or canned clams would work just as well. Likewise, I've included recipes using canned fish and I've indicated where you can instead use leftover cooked fish from a previous recipe. I encourage you to use your creativity and imagination, which will eventually lead to your very own signature dishes!

A Note on Ingredients

Speaking of fresh, frozen, or canned, I've made sure to include recipes that contain ingredients that are easy to find in most grocery stores, no matter where you are. I know from experience that it can be frustrating to be inspired by something you find in a cookbook, only to discover there is an obscure ingredient that you find difficult to source. It takes the fun and spontaneity away from cooking, if you ask me.

A Note on Variations

As for the variations outlined after each main recipe, they are included to offer you some inspiration and to illustrate that recipes are simply guidelines you can follow. With a small change like an aromatic or herb, recipes can transform into an entirely different dish. Cooking should inspire your creativity—it's exploration and experimentation between the foundations of technique and ingredients.

Pan-Seared Salmon with Smoked Paprika and Harissa Carrots, page 23

CHAPTER 1

SALMON

Broiled, roasted, grilled, poached, steamed, smoked, or fried, salmon is the most popular of all the fish we like to eat. It's appealing to many, due to its mild flavor, firm texture, high nutritional value, and gorgeous color, and it's never out of season. Salmon is considered by many to be a powerful superfood. Packed with omega-3 fatty acids, salmon also is chock-full of vitamins and minerals to promote not just heart health but also vision, skin, and brain function.

Many of these recipes are perfectly fit for either fresh salmon or frozen salmon. If you choose frozen salmon, be sure it is thawed completely before preparing. I've even included a few recipes here that use canned salmon.

ROASTED SALMON WITH COMPOUND GARLIC BUTTER

Cooking salmon doesn't get easier than this: Slathering a delicious butter that has been mixed with flavorful ingredients so it creates a sauce as it melts. I keep a few tablespoons in my freezer, so that at any given time, I can toss a knob of it onto cooked pasta, sautéed vegetables, or spread some over toasted baguette. **SERVES 4**

PREP TIME: 20 minutes
COOK TIME: 15 minutes

FOR THE COMPOUND BUTTER

4 tablespoons (½ stick) unsalted butter, at room temperature

2 garlic cloves, minced

Zest of 1 lemon

1 teaspoon whole-grain mustard

1 teaspoon minced fresh flat-leaf parsley

½ teaspoon kosher salt

¼ teaspoon freshly ground black pepper

FOR THE SALMON

12 ounces center-cut salmon fillet, skin on and pin bones removed

1 tablespoon extra-virgin olive oil

Kosher salt

Pinch freshly ground black pepper

1 tablespoon chopped fresh flat-leaf parsley, for garnish

1. Preheat the oven to 400°F.

2. To make the compound butter, in a small bowl, mix together the butter, garlic, lemon zest, mustard, parsley, salt, and pepper until combined. Set aside.

3. To make the salmon, place the fillets in an 8-by-8-inch baking dish and drizzle with the olive oil. Season with salt and pepper and set aside until room temperature, about 20 minutes.

4. Roast for 10 to 12 minutes, until an instant-read thermometer reads 125°F. The flesh should change to opaque pink and, when flaked with a fork, revealing a softer, slightly translucent pink toward the center. Remove the salmon from the oven and, while still hot, spread 2 tablespoons of the compound butter over the top. Sprinkle with the parsley and serve hot.

VARIATION 1 **SALMON WITH CURRY COMPOUND BUTTER:** Try mixing the butter with a couple of teaspoons of curry powder, finely chopped shallots, and a squeeze of lemon juice.

VARIATION 2 **SALMON WITH MISO BUTTER:** Try an Asian-inspired compound butter with 1 teaspoon each of miso paste, grated fresh ginger, finely chopped scallions, and soy sauce.

SALMON WRAPPED IN SEARED RICE WRAP PACKAGES

A version of this dish was served at a dinner party I attended way before I began my culinary career. I remember the buttery salmon was punctuated with the assertive pesto for a balance of texture and flavor I hadn't experienced until that night. What's more, it was all wrapped in a crunchy pouch. Rice wrappers are found in Asian supermarkets. Be sure to allow them to dry slightly to a tacky texture before cooking; this will create a tighter package that holds together. **SERVES 4**

PREP TIME: 20 minutes
COOK TIME: 15 minutes

FOR THE CILANTRO PESTO

½ cup extra-virgin olive oil

½ bunch cilantro, leaves and stems

½ bunch flat-leaf parsley leaves

2 garlic cloves, coarsely chopped

1 tablespoon seasoned rice vinegar

1 teaspoon kosher salt

1 teaspoon ground coriander

Freshly ground black pepper

FOR THE SALMON

4 (3-ounce) salmon fillets, skin and pin bones removed

Kosher salt

Pinch freshly ground black pepper

4 (9-inch) rice paper rounds

2 tablespoons vegetable oil

1. To make the cilantro pesto, in a food processor or blender, process the olive oil, cilantro, parsley, garlic, rice vinegar, salt, coriander, and pepper until smooth but thick. Taste and adjust for seasoning with salt and pepper. Set aside.

2. To make the salmon, lightly season the salmon on both sides with salt and pepper. In a wide shallow pan filled with warm water, soak the rice paper rounds one at a time to soften. When the rice paper is soft and pliable, place it on a clean cutting board.

3. Place one piece of salmon on the lower third of a softened rice paper round. Spread 1 tablespoon of cilantro pesto on top of the salmon. Bring the two opposite sides over to the middle of the salmon, then roll the salmon up, as you would roll a burrito. Set aside and cover with a damp towel to keep the rice wraps from drying out. Repeat the process with the remaining salmon and rice wraps. ❯

4. Heat a large nonstick skillet over medium heat. Add the vegetable oil and swirl to coat the pan. When shimmery wavy lines run through the oil, place the salmon packages in the pan and fry on one side for 5 minutes, or until the rice wraps are brown and crispy. Flip the packages over and fry on the other side for another 5 minutes more until brown and crispy. Serve hot.

VARIATION 1 **WHITEFISH WRAPPED IN SEARED RICE PACKAGES:** You can substitute mackerel, tilapia, catfish, or any mild whitefish, such as cod or snapper, instead of salmon.

VARIATION 2 **ROASTED TOMATO CURRY PESTO:** To make a different pesto, in a blender, pulse a can of drained fire-roasted tomatoes, 2 tablespoons of extra-virgin olive oil, 1 chopped shallot, 1 garlic clove, and 1 tablespoon of curry powder. Spread the mixture over the salmon or any flaky whitefish and proceed with the recipe.

PAN-SEARED SALMON WITH SMOKED PAPRIKA AND HARISSA CARROTS

If you can find rainbow-colored carrots, they contrast beautifully with the color of the salmon, creating a visually appealing dish. Harissa is a bright, hot Moroccan chili paste, so be sure to use it sparingly. If you find the salmon sticking to the bottom of the pan, just leave it alone for a few minutes. The proteins need to sear and form a crust before the fish can be successfully lifted from the pan. **SERVES 4**

PREP TIME: 15 minutes
COOK TIME: 20 minutes

4 (3-ounce) salmon fillets, skin on and pin bones removed

Kosher salt

Freshly ground black pepper

1 tablespoon smoked paprika

4 medium carrots, peeled and sliced ¼ inch thick on the bias

1 lemon, cut into ¼-inch-thick slices

2 tablespoons extra-virgin olive oil

2 teaspoons harissa paste

2 tablespoons vegetable oil or canola oil

1 tablespoon coarsely chopped mint leaves, for garnish

1. Preheat the oven to 400°F. Line a baking sheet with parchment paper or aluminum foil and set aside.

2. Using paper towels, blot each fillet until dry. Season both sides with salt and pepper. Place the fillets skin-side down and sprinkle the smoked paprika over the top. Set aside.

3. In a mixing bowl, toss the carrots, lemon, olive oil, and harissa. Season with salt and pepper. Arrange the mixture on the prepared baking sheet in an even layer and roast for 20 minutes, or until the carrots are tender. If the lemons become slightly caramelized, that's a fantastic bonus!

4. While the carrots are roasting, heat a nonstick skillet over medium-high heat, add the vegetable oil and swirl to coat the pan. When shimmery wavy lines run through the oil, place one fillet skin-side down away from you, so the hot oil doesn't splash you.

5. Gently press down the fish with a spatula for 10 to 15 seconds (this will keep the fish from shrinking too quickly). Repeat this process with the remaining fillets. This will ensure flat, evenly seared fillets. ❯

6. Lower the heat to medium-low and cook for 6 to 7 minutes. Tilt the pan occasionally to redistribute the oil. Sometimes oil settles in the pan and it needs to slip under the salmon to keep the skin cooking to a crispy texture.

7. To see if it's time to flip, insert an instant-read thermometer into the thickest part of the salmon and make sure it reads 120°F. The sides of the fillets should change to opaque pink. Once the opacity is halfway up the sides of the fillets, flip them one at a time. Continue to cook for 1 minute, until the other side is seared.

8. Transfer the fillets, skin-side up, to a clean plate and tent with aluminum foil to rest for a few minutes. Resting helps the fish continue cooking.

9. To serve, place the roasted carrots and lemon on a warm serving platter. Add the salmon, skin-side up, on top. Garnish with the mint.

VARIATION 1 **PAN-SEARED SALMON WITH CUMIN AND MAPLE CARROTS:** Use ground cumin instead of smoked paprika on the salmon and toss the carrots with maple syrup and a pinch of red pepper flakes.

VARIATION 2 **PAN-SEARED SALMON WITH SMOKED PAPRIKA AND BEETS:** Roasted beets and sliced oranges are a nice change from the carrots and lemon. If you can find orange, golden, and pink beets, the color contrast will be amazing. To bump up the spice without adding more heat, add some toasted fennel seeds to complement the beets and orange.

FIRE-ROASTED SALMON WITH HERBS

This is a riff on a well-known recipe Jamie Oliver did on his television series *The Naked Chef*. Mine is simplified. I like to serve this on a bed of sautéed corn kernels with sliced fennel and red bell peppers tossed with arugula. If you don't have a grill, a broiler is a great alternative. **SERVES 4**

PREP TIME: 15 minutes
COOK TIME: 20 minutes

1 pound center-cut salmon fillet, skin on and pin bones removed

2 tablespoons extra-virgin olive oil

Kosher salt

Freshly ground black pepper

2 bunches flat-leaf parsley, leaves and stems

1 bunch cilantro, leaves and stems

1 bunch dill, leaves and stems

2 lemons, each cut into 8 thin slices

1. Heat an outdoor gas grill to medium-high or prepare coals to white ash for a charcoal grill.

2. While the grill is heating, drizzle both sides of the salmon with the olive oil and season with salt and pepper. In a bowl, toss together the parsley, cilantro, and dill. Place half of the herbs in the bottom of a grill basket and lemon slices on top. Place the salmon, skin-side down, and top with the remaining lemon slices, and then the herbs.

3. Close the basket and place it on the grill. Roast for 8 minutes on one side. Flip and roast for another 8 more minutes. Transfer the basket to a baking sheet, tent with aluminum foil, and let it rest for at least 5 minutes.

4. To serve, open the basket, scrape off the top layer of herbs and lemon, and discard. Using a spatula, carefully transfer the herbs and salmon to a serving platter.

VARIATION 1 FIRE-ROASTED SALMON WITH COMPOUND BUTTER AND HERBS: If you still have some leftover compound butter from the Roasted Salmon with Compound Garlic Butter (see page 20), it's a great addition to add before serving.

VARIATION 2 ASIAN-INFUSED FIRE-ROASTED SALMON: Change the flavor profile slightly by using lime and ginger slices and making a bed of lemongrass, parsley, cilantro, and scallions.

SALMON FILLET PROVENÇALE EN PAPILLOTE

Cooking "en papillote" (pronounced "on pap-ee-YOAT") is French for cooking in a parchment pouch. It sounds fancy and complicated, but it's actually very easy. The trick is to get the edges of the parchment sealed tightly to create an airtight environment in which the fish can roast and steam. If using aluminum foil, you can fold the foil in half over the salmon and fold the edges together to create an airtight seal. **SERVES 2**

PREP TIME: 10 minutes
COOK TIME: 15 minutes

2 (3-ounce) salmon fillets, skin on and pin bones removed

Kosher salt

Freshly ground black pepper

3 tablespoons extra-virgin olive oil, divided

¼ cup julienned or shredded carrots

6 cherry tomatoes, halved

6 kalamata olives, pitted and coarsely chopped

1 teaspoon finely chopped shallot

1 teaspoon minced fresh flat-leaf parsley

1. Preheat the oven to 400°F. Fold a 12 × 18 inch sheet of parchment paper in half and draw a half-heart shape, starting at the inside of the fold. Using scissors, cut along the edges to create the heart shape.

2. Open the heart and place the salmon in the center of one side of the heart. Generously season with salt and pepper and drizzle with 1 tablespoon of olive oil. Set aside.

3. In a small bowl, toss together the carrots, tomatoes, olives, shallot, and parsley with 1 tablespoon of olive oil. Divide the vegetables and place one half on top of the salmon fillet. Gently fold the other half of the parchment heart over the salmon so the edges line up. Repeat with the other fillet.

4. Starting at the curved end of the heart, make one folded crease, about ¼ inch from the edge. Continue to make successive folds along the edge of the package, making sure each new fold starts from the center of the previous one; the folds should overlap. This will keep the salmon sealed during cooking.

5. When you reach the pointed end, fold up the paper, then fold it back and tuck it underneath the package. Repeat this process with another sheet of parchment, and the remaining fillet and vegetables.

6. Transfer the packages to a baking sheet, drizzle the remaining 1 tablespoon of olive oil over the top of each one, and use your fingertips to spread the oil over the packages.

7. Bake for 10 minutes, or until the packages are browned and puffy.

8. Remove the packages from the oven and let them rest for a couple of minutes. They will start to deflate. Carefully cut around the edges to open the package. Transfer the salmon to a plate. Spoon the vegetables and any sauce drippings from the package on top. Serve immediately.

VARIATION 1 ASIAN-STYLE SALMON EN PAPILLOTE: By using lemongrass, ginger, sliced chiles, lime, and cilantro, you get a lovely Thai-inspired salmon en papillote.

VARIATION 2 MEDITERRANEAN SALMON EN PAPILLOTE: A simple Mediterranean mix of flavors works well here, too. Spread sliced fennel, orange zest, pitted black olives, fresh thyme, and oregano over top of the fish.

SALMON TERIYAKI

Restaurant versions of this dish tend to be on the sweeter side with lots of added sugar or corn syrup. The sauce also can be made thick and gravy-like by the addition of cornstarch. Here, we celebrate Japanese teriyaki sauce in its purest and simplest form: just three ingredients, plus the addition of some grated ginger. This one is for my dear friend's son, Cooper. He's a big fan of salmon teriyaki, and my hope is that he will make this for his parents someday. **SERVES 4**

PREP TIME: 20 minutes
COOK TIME: 15 minutes

½ cup sake

¼ cup mirin

¼ cup soy sauce

½ teaspoon grated peeled fresh ginger

4 (3-ounce) salmon fillets, skin on and pin bones removed

Kosher salt

Freshly ground black pepper

2 tablespoons vegetable oil or canola oil

1½ cups cooked white rice, for serving

1 teaspoon toasted sesame seeds, for garnish

1 scallion, thinly sliced, for garnish (white and green parts)

1. In a small bowl, whisk together the sake, mirin, soy sauce, and ginger. Set aside.

2. Season the salmon on both sides with salt and pepper.

3. Heat a medium nonstick skillet over medium-high heat. Add the vegetable oil and swirl to coat the pan. When shimmery wavy lines run through the oil, place the salmon in the pan, skin-side down, and sear for 6 minutes. Tilt the pan occasionally to redistribute the oil as the salmon cooks. Gently flip the salmon over and cook the other side for 2 minutes. Add more oil, 1 teaspoon at a time, if needed.

4. Transfer the salmon to a clean plate and, using a paper towel, wipe the oil from the skillet. Pour the prepared sauce into the skillet and bring to a boil over medium-high heat. Cook until the sauce has reduced by one-third, about 3 minutes.

5. Return the salmon to the pan, skin-side up, and spoon the reduced sauce over top. Keep cooking for another 2 minutes, until an instant-read thermometer inserted into the thickest part of the fish reads 125°F. The flesh should change to opaque pink and, when flaked with a fork, reveal a softer, slightly translucent pink toward the center.

6. Divide the rice between four plates. Place the salmon on top of each. Spoon the excess sauce from the pan over the salmon and rice. Garnish with the sesame seeds and scallions and serve.

VARIATION 1 WHITEFISH TERIYAKI: Substitute mackerel or catfish instead of salmon. This teriyaki sauce even goes great with beef and chicken.

VARIATION 2 SALMON TERIYAKI SALAD: Flake the cooked salmon teriyaki over torn butter lettuce leaves. Top the salad with sliced avocado, cucumber slices, and a drizzle of ginger-sesame vinaigrette. To make the dressing, mix together 3 tablespoons of vegetable oil, 2 tablespoons of rice vinegar, 1 tablespoon of sesame oil, 1 teaspoon of grated fresh ginger, and ½ teaspoon of mustard.

SALMON ONIGIRI

Sometimes we crave a satisfying snack that isn't laden with sugar or deep-fried. Onigiri is the perfect snack for such an occasion. Onigiri can be packed with assertive and flavorful fillings, like umeboshi plums, pickled daikon, or salty fish. Here, I choose to use canned salmon. To enhance the flavor and texture of the salmon, we cook it with some mirin and soy sauce to achieve a sweet-salty balance and a crispy texture. **SERVES 2**

PREP TIME: 20 minutes
COOK TIME: 10 minutes

2 teaspoons vegetable oil or canola oil

1 (6-ounce) can boneless, skinless salmon, drained

2 teaspoons mirin or seasoned rice vinegar

1 teaspoon soy sauce

1 tablespoon furikake

3 cups cooked short-grain rice (sushi rice preferred)

Kosher salt

2 tablespoons toasted sesame seeds

1 sheet nori seaweed, cut into 4 strips

1. In a small skillet, heat the oil over medium heat. When shimmery wavy lines run through the oil, add the salmon, mirin, and soy sauce. Gently sauté, breaking up the salmon and mixing it with the sauce, for 5 minutes, until the sauce has been absorbed and the salmon is slightly crispy. Transfer to a small bowl and set aside to cool. When cooled, fold in the furikake.

2. Lightly season the cooked rice with salt. Fold in the salmon mixture and sesame seeds. Divide the rice mixture into four equal balls. Wet your hands with cold water and roll one of the balls into an egg shape. Wrap one strip of nori around the middle of the egg and place on a serving plate. Repeat the process with the remaining rice and nori.

3. Serve immediately or keep wrapped in plastic wrap at room temperature for up to 2 hours.

VARIATION 1 TUNA, MACKEREL, OR FRIED SHRIMP ONIGIRI: You can substitute canned tuna, mackerel, or fried shrimp in onigiri. Your imagination and creativity are the only limits.

VARIATION 2 SALMON MUSUBI: In Hawaii, Spam musubi is a very popular snack. If Spam isn't your jam, try using salmon as a filling instead. You can assemble the onigiri components to make a salmon musubi by dividing the rice into two oval patties. Layer the salmon filling in between the patties and wrap the nori around the whole thing.

GRAVLAX

Curing fish was one of the many methods used to preserve it before the invention of the refrigerator. Enhanced flavors and new textures are bonuses to this preserving method. Gravlax is the easiest and quickest method, using a simple mix of salt, sugar, and a few spices for extra flavor and allowing time and osmosis to do the work. If you can't find juniper berries, substitute with yellow mustard seeds. **SERVES 6 TO 8**

PREP TIME: 15 minutes, plus 3 days to cure

1 (8 ounce) salmon fillet, skin on and pin bones removed

1 teaspoon whole black peppercorns

1 teaspoon whole juniper berries

1½ tablespoons kosher salt

1½ tablespoons sugar

1 tablespoon coarsely chopped fresh dill

2 tablespoons freshly squeezed lemon juice

1 tablespoon gin or vodka

1. Rinse the salmon under cold water and blot dry with paper towels. Place the salmon, skin-side down, in the baking dish.

2. With a mortar and pestle, coarsely crack the peppercorns and juniper berries a few times. In a small bowl, mix the spices with the salt, sugar, dill, lemon juice, and gin.

3. Spread the spice mixture over the top of the salmon and cover with plastic wrap. Refrigerate for 3 days undisturbed.

4. Remove the gravlax from the baking dish and rinse off the curing mixture. Blot dry with paper towels.

5. Using a sharp knife, slice the gravlax into paper-thin slices and serve cold. The gravlax can be stored in the refrigerator tightly wrapped in plastic for up to 5 days.

VARIATION 1 JALAPEÑO GRAVLAX: Add a teaspoon of minced fresh jalapeño and cilantro instead of the dill for a spicy twist.

VARIATION 2 FAUX SMOKED GRAVLAX: Substitute brown sugar for the granulated sugar and add a drop of liquid smoke to get a smoked salmon effect without actually smoking!

Spicy Tuna Poke, page 37

CHAPTER 2

TUNA

Tuna, especially canned tuna, is the second most popular fish available for people to eat, from classic comfort food recipes to more adventurous dishes. In the 1950s, tuna became America's favorite fish and was dubbed the "chicken of the sea," due to the canning industry's ability to remove the fishy taste in its canning process, making it more palatable and incredibly inexpensive. Since then, canned tuna's most popular use is as an add-in food for salads, sandwiches, and casseroles.

Buying fresh tuna may be a little luxurious for its price, but it's worth it. When buying fresh tuna from the market, look for wild-caught tuna, such as albacore, yellowfin, and skipjack. Skipjack tuna, the smallest of the species, is in larger supply and has the lowest amounts of mercury. A fresh tuna steak is deep dark red in color and has an almost translucent quality to its flesh. When cooked, it has a deliciously meaty flavor to it, rich and oily and deeply satisfying.

As for canned tuna, pay close attention to the words on the labels to give you important information on the texture, what it is packed in (opt for oil-packed for the best flavor), and what kind of tuna is in the can, for sustainability reasons.

TUNA NOODLE CASSEROLE

The king of comfort food, baked tuna casserole has been an American staple since the 1950s. Developed for growing families using inexpensive processed ingredients, it is an efficient meal in which protein, vegetable, and starch are served together in one dish. This recipe satisfies a comfort food craving without using canned processed soup as the base. It's slightly more work, but really worth it in the end. **SERVES 4 TO 6**

PREP TIME: 15 minutes
COOK TIME: 55 minutes

8 ounces extra-wide dried egg noodles

3 tablespoons kosher salt, plus more for seasoning

6 tablespoons (¾ stick) unsalted butter, melted and divided

2 cups white mushrooms, washed well and cut into ¼-inch-thick slices

½ small yellow onion, chopped

2 celery stalks, cut into ¼-inch dice

2 tablespoons dry sherry

Freshly ground black pepper

4 tablespoons all-purpose flour

¾ cup whole milk

¾ cup low-sodium chicken stock ❯

1. Bring a large pot of water to a boil over medium-high heat. Add the noodles and the salt and cook according to package instructions until tender, about 6 minutes. Drain and set aside.

2. While the noodles are cooking, preheat the oven to 375°F. Brush 2 tablespoons of melted butter all over the inside of a 9-by-13-inch baking dish. Set aside.

3. In a large sauté pan or skillet, heat the remaining 4 tablespoons of butter over medium-high heat. Add the mushrooms and a pinch of salt and cook until the mushrooms are golden brown, about 8 minutes. Add the onion and celery and sauté for 4 minutes, until softened.

4. Lower the heat to medium-low and add the sherry. Stir briefly and cook until the sherry has dried. Season with salt and pepper. Add the flour and stir until the vegetables are coated.

5. Add the milk and stock and stir for about 2 minutes, until the sauce thickens. Remove from the heat and gently fold in the tuna and parsley until combined. Transfer the tuna mixture to a bowl and fold in the cooked egg noodles. Transfer to the prepared baking dish.

2 (7-ounce) cans
oil-packed solid albacore
tuna, oil drained
and reserved

2 tablespoons finely
chopped fresh
flat-leaf parsley

½ cup panko bread crumbs

6. In a small bowl, mix together 1 tablespoon of reserved tuna oil, the bread crumbs, and a pinch of salt. Sprinkle the bread crumb mixture on top of the casserole.

7. Bake for 35 minutes, or until the casserole is bubbling and the topping is golden brown.

VARIATION 1 ASIAN-INSPIRED SALMON CASSEROLE: Use canned salmon instead of tuna and add shiitake mushrooms, ginger, and edamame. Flavor with a dash of soy sauce in chicken stock instead of milk. After the casserole has baked, sprinkle furikake over the bread crumbs and enjoy!

VARIATION 2 STUFFED TUNA SHELLS: Do a take on stuffed shells by mixing in some ricotta cheese with the casserole filling and stuff them into jumbo cooked pasta shells. Sprinkle with the bread crumb mixture before baking.

TUNA AND WHITE BEAN SALAD

This salad reminds me of my previous career as a campaign consultant. Our office manager prepared lunch every day for all of us at the campaign office, and I would always look forward to lunches that included tuna. Thank you, Sharman, for feeding us to victory (we won that election, by the way). **SERVES 4**

PREP TIME: 10 minutes, plus 30 minutes to overnight to chill

1 (15-ounce) can cannellini beans, drained and rinsed

1 (7-ounce) can oil-packed solid albacore tuna, oil drained and reserved

2 celery stalks, cut into ¼-inch-thick strips on the bias

1 cup loosely packed coarsely chopped fresh flat-leaf parsley

1 tablespoon finely chopped shallot

1 lemon, zested then halved

Kosher salt

Freshly ground black pepper

2 to 3 tablespoons extra-virgin olive oil

1 tablespoon white balsamic vinegar

2 large handfuls baby kale or arugula, coarsely chopped

Crackers, crostini, or flatbread, for serving

1. In a large bowl, combine the beans, tuna, celery, parsley, shallot, and lemon zest. Season with salt and pepper. Using a wooden spoon, gently break up the fish into small chunks and mash a few of the beans.

2. Juice half the lemon. Add the lemon juice, olive oil, and vinegar, then gently fold in the kale or arugula. Season with salt and pepper. If the salad is still a bit dry, drizzle a bit of the oil reserved from the tuna can.

3. Cover and refrigerate for 30 minutes or overnight. Serve cold or at room temperature with crackers.

VARIATION 1 **SALMON AND WHITE BEAN SALAD:** Canned salmon goes well with this salad, too. Swap 1 (6-ounce) can of boneless, skinless salmon for the tuna for a whole new flavorful meal.

VARIATION 2 **TUNA AND CHICKPEA SALAD:** If you have canned tuna, canned beans, some assertive aromatics, and some greens, you have the makings of an amazing salad. Consider adding some sliced olives, chickpeas, cherry tomatoes, and arugula to the salad instead of kale.

SPICY TUNA POKE

A chopped salad of raw tuna for dinner is the perfect meal on a hot summer night. Poke is now very popular here on the mainland, even though it's been a staple in Hawaii for generations, and for good reason: It's simple to make and delicious as an appetizer or a light meal. Make sure you select the finest quality ahi tuna your budget allows. This is not the recipe to skimp on and go for something less. **SERVES 4**

PREP TIME: 15 minutes

1½ tablespoons soy sauce

2 teaspoons sesame oil

1 teaspoon honey

1 teaspoon sriracha

12 ounces raw sushi-grade ahi tuna, cut into ½-inch cubes

3 scallions, thinly sliced (white and green parts)

Kosher salt

Freshly ground black pepper

1 tablespoon furikake

1. In a medium bowl, whisk together the soy sauce, sesame oil, honey, and sriracha.

2. Fold in the tuna and scallions, then season with salt and pepper. Transfer to a chilled serving bowl and sprinkle the furikake on top. Serve immediately.

VARIATION 1 SPICY TUNA POKE BOWLS: Add the poke to a bowl of cooked white rice, sliced vegetables, diced avocado, and edamame and boom: poke rice bowls! Also, there is no such thing as too much furikake.

VARIATION 2 SPICY SALMON POKE: Raw sushi-grade salmon makes an excellent protein for poke as well.

OPEN-FACED TUNA MELTS

My best friend and I have been meeting for lunch on occasion for nearly 20 years. For the first couple of years, we would head to The Village Grill, a coffee shop in the West Portal neighborhood of San Francisco, and he would faithfully order a tuna melt each time. Over the years, we've moved around the Bay Area and still meet up for lunch—only now "meeting for tuna melts" has become our code for "lunch." **SERVES 2**

PREP TIME: 10 minutes
COOK TIME: 10 minutes

2 tablespoons
unsalted butter, at
room temperature

2 sourdough bread slices

1 (7-ounce) can
oil-packed solid albacore
tuna, drained

½ cup quartered
grape tomatoes

1 celery stalk,
finely chopped

½ small shallot,
finely chopped

3 tablespoons mayonnaise

1 tablespoon coarsely
chopped fresh flat-leaf
parsley, divided

1 teaspoon Dijon mustard

Kosher salt

Freshly ground
black pepper

2 Swiss cheese slices

1. Line a baking sheet with aluminum foil and set a non-stick skillet over medium heat.

2. While the pan is heating, spread the butter on one side of each slice of bread and place in the pan, butter-side down.

3. Cook until the the bread is a crispy golden color, about 3 minutes. Transfer the slices, crispy-side down, to the prepared baking sheet.

4. Preheat the broiler.

5. In a medium bowl, mix together the tuna, tomatoes, celery, shallot, mayonnaise, all but a pinch of the parsley, mustard, salt, and pepper.

6. Divide the tuna mixture between the slices of bread and spread evenly. Top each with a slice of cheese.

7. Broil for 1 minute, or until the cheese begins to melt and browns slightly.

8. Garnish with the remaining pinch of parsley, transfer to plates, and serve immediately.

VARIATION 1 **BAGEL TUNA MELT:** Since bagels are thicker and denser than sliced sourdough bread, it may take a bit longer to toast in step 1. Conversely, an English muffin is thinner and lighter and will need less time.

VARIATION 2 **SHRIMP OR CRAB MELTS:** Cooked shrimp or cooked crab goes great in these melts as well. Use Monterey Jack cheese in place of the Swiss.

MANGO-GLAZED TUNA STEAKS

This would be a good recipe to pull out if you are trying to impress folks with your cooking. It provides you with a perfectly balanced sweet, savory, and spicy glaze that, when broiled, gives off a deep lacquered finish with a restaurant-quality appeal. **SERVES 4**

PREP TIME: 10 minutes
COOK TIME: 15 minutes

1 cup chopped fresh or frozen mango

1 (1-inch) piece fresh ginger, peeled and minced

½ shallot, finely chopped

1 garlic clove, smashed

2 teaspoons rice vinegar

2 teaspoons soy sauce

1 teaspoon honey

½ teaspoon sriracha

Kosher salt

Freshly ground black pepper

4 (3.5-ounce) tuna steaks

2 tablespoons vegetable or canola oil

2 tablespoons coarsely chopped fresh cilantro leaves, for garnish

1. Preheat the oven to 425°F. Line a baking sheet with aluminum foil and set aside.

2. In a blender or food processor, combine the mango, ginger, shallot, garlic, vinegar, soy sauce, honey, and sriracha. Blend until smooth. Season with salt and pepper.

3. Place the tuna steaks on the prepared baking sheet and drizzle the oil over both sides. Season both sides with salt and pepper.

4. Brush the mango glaze on both sides of the tuna, then roast for 5 minutes. Flip the fish over and brush again with the mango glaze. Roast for another 5 minutes, or until the tuna is pink and rare inside.

5. Remove the pan from the oven and turn on the broiler. Brush the tops of the fish again with the glaze and broil for 2 minutes, until the glaze starts to brown slightly.

6. Transfer the tuna to plates and garnish with the cilantro. Serve hot.

VARIATION 1 MANGO-GLAZED FISH: Salmon, tilapia, and even catfish fillets work beautifully with this mango glaze.

VARIATION 2 TUNA WITH MANGO SALSA: Instead of purée-ing them, dice the mango and ginger and add ½ cup of diced red bell pepper. Broil the fish as instructed and serve the salsa directly on top of the fish.

OIL-POACHED TUNA

If oil-poaching is new to you, I encourage you to embrace this cooking method, particularly for fish. In this recipe, the tuna's flavor is fully infused with the aromatics. I like to poach the tuna, then use the cooked fish and oil in salads and pastas. Before you reach for another can of tuna, give this recipe a try. **SERVES 4**

PREP TIME: 10 minutes
COOK TIME: 15 minutes

3 cups extra-virgin olive oil

4 large garlic
cloves, smashed

2 strips lemon zest

1 fresh bay leaf

Pinch red pepper flakes

4 (3.5-ounce) tuna fillets

Kosher salt

Pinch freshly ground
black pepper

1. In a shallow saucepan wide enough to fit the tuna fillets, heat the oil, garlic, lemon zest, bay leaf, and red pepper flakes over medium-low heat until the garlic starts to sizzle slightly.

2. Season both sides of the tuna with salt and pepper. Using a slotted spoon, place the tuna in the oil. Add more oil if the fish isn't fully submerged by at least 1/2 inch. Cook until the tuna is opaque, about 9 minutes, flipping the fillets halfway through cooking. If the tuna is slightly pink in the center, that's fine; medium-rare tuna has a great texture.

3. Using a slotted spoon, transfer the tuna to a plate lined with paper towels. Allow the tuna to cool slightly before serving.

VARIATION 1 SPICED OIL-POACHED TUNA: Use whole dried chiles and cracked whole spices—such as cumin, coriander, and allspice—in the poaching oil.

VARIATION 2 OIL-POACHED SALMON OR MACKEREL: You can oil-poach any fish or shrimp you like! Salmon and mackerel are especially friendly to oil-poaching.

TUNA AND TOMATOES WITH SPAGHETTI

I know how it can be, friend. You come home, tired and hungry after a long day at work, and the thought of having to cook a meal is overwhelming. However, the time it takes to boil water and cook the pasta is all the time you need to get something delicious and satisfying on the table with this easy recipe. **SERVES 4**

PREP TIME: 10 minutes
COOK TIME: 20 minutes

8 ounces linguine

1 (6-ounce) can oil-packed solid albacore tuna, oil drained and reserved

1 large shallot, cut into ¼-inch dice

½ teaspoon red pepper flakes

Kosher salt

6 Roma tomatoes, seeded and chopped

½ cup coarsely chopped pitted green olives

1 tablespoon coarsely chopped fresh flat-leaf parsley, for garnish

Extra-virgin olive oil, for drizzling

1. Bring a large pot of water to a boil over medium-high heat. Add the pasta and cook according to package instructions until tender, about 10 minutes. Reserve 1 cup of pasta water, then drain and set aside.

2. In sauté pan or skillet over medium-high heat, heat 2 tablespoons of the reserved tuna oil. Add the shallot, red pepper flakes, and a pinch of salt and sauté for 4 minutes, or until the shallot is translucent.

3. Add the tomatoes and gently crush them with the back of a wooden spoon. Continue to cook until the tomatoes break down, about 4 minutes.

4. Lower the heat to medium and add the olives. Simmer for another 2 minutes, then gently fold in the tuna.

5. Transfer the pasta back to the stockpot. Add the tomato sauce and toss to coat. Use a splash or two of the pasta water to loosen up the sauce, if needed.

6. To serve, divide the pasta and sauce among four warm pasta bowls. Garnish with the parsley and a drizzle of olive oil.

VARIATION 1 OIL-POACHED TUNA AND TOMATO PASTA: Remember that recipe for Oil-Poached Tuna (see page 41)? This would be a perfect use for any leftovers. Just crumble it right into the sauce.

VARIATION 2 ONE-POT TUNA PASTA: A one-pot version of this would save on the dishes. Instead of cooking the pasta separately, cook the sauce ingredients in a large Dutch oven. When the sauce is cooked, add the pasta and 2 cups of hot water. Cover the pot and cook over medium heat for about 15 minutes, or until the pasta is al dente.

TUNA AND SUMMER VEGETABLE KABOBS WITH CHIMICHURRI SAUCE

Tuna steaks and assorted vegetables with a vibrant green sauce on a plate—sounds lovely, but boring, right? Rearrange the fish and vegetables by threading them onto skewers and and grill them. Suddenly, they are much more appealing and delicious. Use a grill pan or broil them if you don't have access to an outdoor grill. **SERVES 4**

PREP TIME: 15 minutes
COOK TIME: 10 minutes

FOR THE CHIMICHURRI SAUCE

½ cup extra-virgin olive oil

1 bunch flat-leaf parsley leaves

½ bunch cilantro, leaves and stems

½ shallot, coarsely chopped

2 tablespoons red wine vinegar

1 large garlic clove, smashed

1 teaspoon ground cumin

Pinch red pepper flakes

Kosher salt

Freshly ground black pepper ❯

1. To make the chimichurri sauce, in a blender, combine the olive oil, parsley, cilantro, shallot, vinegar, garlic, cumin, and red pepper flakes. Season with salt and pepper and process until smooth. Alternatively, finely mince the shallots, garlic, and herbs and stir the remaining ingredients together for a chunkier sauce.

2. To make the kabobs, in a large bowl, combine the tuna, tomatoes, zucchini, squash, onion, and bell pepper. Toss with the olive oil and season with salt and pepper until well coated.

3. On metal skewers, thread the fish and vegetables so that each kabob has evenly alternating pieces of tuna, zucchini, squash, onion, bell pepper, and tomato. Lightly season with salt and pepper. Transfer to a large platter and refrigerate, covered, until ready to grill or overnight.

4. Heat an outdoor gas grill to medium-high or prepare coals to white ash for a charcoal grill.

FOR THE KABOBS

12 ounces tuna steak, cut into 12 equal cubes

8 cherry tomatoes

2 zucchini, cut crosswise into 1-inch chunks

2 yellow squash, cut crosswise into 1-inch chunks

1 large red onion, cut into 1-inch chunks

1 large orange bell pepper, cut into 1-inch chunks

3 tablespoons extra-virgin olive oil

Kosher salt

Freshly ground black pepper

5. Arrange the kabobs across the grill and lower the heat to medium-low. If you are cooking over charcoal, move the charcoal to one side of the grill and place the kabobs on the grill so that the heat source is next to the kabobs. Cover the grill and cook for 3 minutes, or until the underside of the skewers begin to show grill marks. Turn the skewers and grill on the other side for 3 minutes.

6. Turn the grill off and keep it covered. On a charcoal grill, transfer the kabobs to a baking sheet and tent with aluminum foil. Let the skewers rest for 3 more minutes so that the tuna continues to cook to medium rare.

7. Transfer the kabobs to a warm platter and drizzle the chimichurri sauce over top. Serve immediately.

VARIATION 1 **SALMON AND VEGETABLE KABOBS WITH CHIMICHURRI SAUCE:** If you want to substitute a slightly flakier fish than tuna, like salmon, it's easier to skewer if the fish is slightly frozen. After cutting them into chunks, transfer to a plate and place in the freezer for 20 to 30 minutes, or until the fish is barely frozen but not frozen solid. The fish will thaw quickly as you prepare the skewers.

VARIATION 2 **SHRIMP SKEWERS WITH SEASONAL VEGETABLES AND HERB SAUCE:** Extra jumbo shrimp (U16/20) goes beautifully with the vegetables and sauce. Mix up the vegetables with what's available: cremini mushrooms, fennel wedges, chunks of scallion, cauliflower florets—anything is possible! If cilantro is not your thing, try a blended sauce of rosemary, thyme, and basil with lemon juice instead of red wine vinegar.

Sardines with Pasta, Pine Nuts, and Red Pepper, page 53

CHAPTER 3

SARDINES

You either love them or you hate them. If sardines aren't your favorite, I'm going to say that you haven't been properly introduced. Small, plentiful, tasty, high in protein and omega-3 fatty acids, and low in mercury, sardines are a great way to introduce more fish into your diet. Consider how budget-friendly they are, too. They are so small and convenient to add to an already familiar dish and morph it into something new.

If you're only familiar with the canned sardines, give the fresh ones a try. Larger ones can be split open, backbone removed, then grilled lightly. Salt, lemon juice, and some fresh herbs bring out the best of the sardine's flavors. Eat the bones and skin, as these parts are packed with nutrients, too.

Sadly, there are no sardine canneries in the United States anymore, as the last one in Maine closed in 2010. Despite the lack of domestic sardines, you can still find sustainable sardines (canned or fresh) originating from Spain, Italy, and Japan.

SARDINES ON TOAST

This is a very simple recipe utilizing canned sardines and a small jar of diced pimentos. It's perfect for a light lunch, an afternoon snack, or as an appetizer for a large party. Be sure to select sardines packed in olive oil for the best flavor and because the recipe calls for using the oil from the can. **SERVES 4**

PREP TIME: 10 minutes
COOK TIME: 10 minutes

4 rustic sourdough bread slices

1 (4.5-ounce) can oil-packed sardines, oil drained and reserved

1 garlic clove, peeled

1 (2-ounce) jar diced pimentos, drained

Kosher salt

Freshly ground black pepper

Juice of ½ lemon

1 tablespoon minced fresh flat-leaf parsley, for garnish

1. Brush both sides of the bread with the reserved sardine oil. In a small skillet over medium heat, toast the bread, flipping once, until the bread is golden brown, about 3 minutes per side. It should be crispy but still chewy in the center. Rub the tops of the toast gently with the garlic. Mince the remainder of the garlic and set aside.

2. In the same skillet, heat 1 teaspoon of the reserved sardine oil over medium heat. Add the sardines, pimento, and minced garlic. Season with salt and pepper, and sauté, stirring, until the sardines are just warmed through.

3. Drizzle the lemon juice over the sardines and arrange on the toasts. Garnish with the parsley and serve warm.

VARIATION 1 SMOKY SPANISH SARDINES ON TOAST: Add a pinch of smoked paprika and a drizzle of sherry vinegar instead of lemon juice for a smoky Spanish tapa.

VARIATION 2 BEANS AND SARDINES ON TOAST: Are you familiar with the popular English snack beans on toast? Add a drained can of white beans to the skillet when you are sautéing the pimentos and garlic. Gently smash the beans so that they become a spreadable consistency, and spread over the toast before warming up the sardines. Yummy.

SARDINES WITH WHITE BEANS AND PEPPERS

During my college years, I spent many hours eschewing schoolwork to watch cooking shows on our local PBS channel. I remember one recipe in particular from Jacques Pépin: a salad with sardines and red bell peppers. I was too broke to order the companion cookbook at the time, so I had to recreate the salad from memory. Over the years, I've refined and tweaked it. Today, it's one of my husband's favorite salads. **SERVES 4**

PREP TIME: 10 minutes
COOK TIME: 10 minutes

3 tablespoons extra-virgin olive oil, or oil drained from the sardine can, divided

1 large red bell pepper, cut into ¼-inch-thick strips

Kosher salt

Freshly ground black pepper

3 garlic cloves, minced

1 (15-ounce) can cannellini beans, drained and rinsed

2 teaspoons smoked paprika

1 (4.5-ounce) can oil-packed sardines, oil drained and reserved

1 tablespoon sherry vinegar or red wine vinegar

2 large handfuls baby kale or wild arugula

1. Heat a nonstick skillet over medium heat. Add 2 tablespoons of olive oil and swirl to coat the pan. When shimmery wavy lines run through the oil, add the peppers and sauté for 4 minutes, or until they begin to soften. Season with salt and pepper.

2. Add the garlic and sauté for a few seconds more. Add the beans and paprika and sauté for 2 minutes, or until the beans start to brown slightly.

3. Add the sardines and toss gently to combine, breaking up the sardines into smaller chunks. Keep folding gently until the sardines are warmed through.

4. Remove the pan from the heat and allow it to cool slightly. Add the vinegar and kale, seasoning with a pinch more salt and pepper. The heat from the beans and vegetables should wilt the kale slightly. Drizzle the remaining 1 tablespoon of oil over the salad and serve warm.

VARIATION 1 SMOKED MACKEREL WITH WHITE BEANS: Smoked mackerel in a can is excellent in this salad as well. Instead of using kale or arugula, toss in handfuls of frisée or baby lettuce.

VARIATION 2 SARDINES WITH WHITE BEANS AND OLIVES: Round out the salad by adding ½ cup of pitted olives and ¼ cup of sliced almonds for a little crunch.

SARDINES A LA PLANCHA WITH FENNEL AND OLIVES

In Spanish, "a la Plancha" means "to sear on a hot flat metal surface." Seek out fresh sardines for this recipe. It's totally worth it. Because of their small size, the fish cook quickly and don't have that annoying tendency to dry out. Fresh sardines are rich and flavorful and need a bright, assertive salad to serve as their counterpoint. **SERVES 4**

PREP TIME: 15 minutes
COOK TIME: 10 minutes

4 fresh sardines, butterflied and boned

Kosher salt

Freshly ground black pepper

¼ cup extra-virgin olive oil, divided

1 tablespoon freshly squeezed lemon juice

1 fennel bulb, trimmed and thinly sliced, fronds reserved for garnish

½ cup halved pitted green olives

Zest and juice of 1 navel orange

2 tablespoons coarsely chopped fresh flat-leaf parsley

1. Place the sardines on a plate and season both sides with salt and pepper. Drizzle with 2 tablespoons of olive oil.

2. Heat a cast iron skillet or griddle over medium-high heat until it begins to smoke. Place the sardines in the pan and sear for 6 minutes, flipping them halfway through. Drizzle the lemon juice over the sardines, transfer to a platter, and tent with aluminum foil to keep warm.

3. In a mixing bowl, toss the fennel, olives, orange zest, and parsley. Season with salt and pepper. Add 1 tablespoon of orange juice and the remaining 2 tablespoons of olive oil and toss to coat.

4. Transfer the salad to a serving platter and place the sardines on top. Garnish with fennel fronds and serve immediately.

VARIATION 1 SMOKY GRILLED SARDINES AND FENNEL: Grill the sardines and fennel slices before adding to the salad. The smoky flavor adds another layer to this delicious meal.

VARIATION 2 WHITEFISH WITH FENNEL AND OLIVES: This salad will be just as delicious using trout, tilapia, or mackerel.

SARDINES AND HORSERADISH (SMØRREBRØD)

Smørrebrød are Scandinavian open-faced sandwiches made with seeded rye bread and butter topped with assorted ingredients, such as vegetables, cheese, meat, or fish. They are usually enjoyed during lunch or as an afternoon snack. On a recent trip to Denmark, our host took us to a traditional smørrebrød restaurant for lunch, where herring was the main fish served. But here, sardines can do the trick, too. **SERVES 2**

PREP TIME: 15 minutes
COOK TIME: 10 minutes

1 shallot, cut crosswise into thin rings

¼ cup red wine vinegar

2 tablespoons Dijon mustard

1 teaspoon prepared horseradish

4 seeded rye bread slices, toasted

1 large handful baby spinach leaves

2 (4.5-ounce) cans oil-packed sardines, oil drained and reserved

Kosher salt

Freshly ground black pepper

1. In a small bowl, soak the shallot in the vinegar.

2. In a small bowl, mix together the mustard and horseradish. On each slice of toast, spread the mustard and horseradish evenly and top each with spinach. Set aside on plates.

3. In a small nonstick skillet over medium heat, add 2 teaspoons of the reserved sardine oil and swirl to coat the pan. When shimmery wavy lines run through the oil, add the sardines and fry for 3 minutes on each side, flipping once, until crispy.

4. Divide the sardines between the pieces of toast and top with the pickled shallot rings. Season with salt and pepper and serve.

VARIATION 1 SARDINES WITH HARDBOILED EGGS: Add a layer of sliced hardboiled egg to the smørrebrød.

VARIATION 2 SARDINES WITH CUCUMBERS AND DILL: Add a layer of thinly sliced cucumbers to the toast before assembling the rest of the toppings. Garnish with chopped dill.

FISHERMAN'S BREAKFAST

I eat eggs for breakfast only on days that end in "y." I'm constantly on the hunt for new and interesting ways to cook, serve, and enjoy eggs. This recipe is one of my favorites. A fisherman's breakfast is similar to corned beef hash, except it is served with sardines instead. **SERVES 4**

PREP TIME: 10 minutes
COOK TIME: 25 minutes

2 (4.5-ounce) cans oil-packed sardines, oil drained and reserved

2 Roma tomatoes, cut into ¼-inch dice

1 small red onion, cut into ¼-inch dice

1 small pasilla pepper, cut into ¼-inch dice

3 garlic cloves, minced

1 tablespoon capers, rinsed and chopped

Kosher salt

Freshly ground black pepper

2 large eggs

1 tablespoon chopped fresh dill, for garnish

1. Preheat the oven to 400°F. Place a 10-inch cast iron skillet in the oven.

2. In a mixing bowl, break the sardines into chunks. Mix in the tomatoes, onion, pasilla pepper, garlic, and capers, until thoroughly combined. Season with salt and pepper and add 2 tablespoons of reserved sardine oil.

3. Transfer the mixture to the skillet and bake for 15 minutes.

4. Remove the pan from the oven. Using the back of a large kitchen spoon, make two shallow depressions in the mixture. Crack an egg into each depression and season with salt and pepper. Continue to bake for another 8 minutes, or until the eggs have just set.

5. Remove the pan from the oven and tent with aluminum foil, resting for 2 to 3 minutes. Garnish with the chopped dill and serve immediately.

VARIATION 1 FRESH SARDINE FISHERMAN'S BREAKFAST: If you would like to use fresh sardines, cut them into bite-size chunks and mix them in raw with the vegetables. Let the mixture cook for 5 minutes more before adding the eggs.

VARIATION 2 LEFTOVER FISHERMAN'S BREAKFAST: Substitute any cooked fish you have on hand. Trout, mackerel, or tuna—add some cooked diced potatoes or a can of white beans to bulk up the breakfast.

SARDINES WITH PASTA, PINE NUTS, AND RED PEPPER

In the amount of time it takes for the water to boil and for the pasta to cook, the rest of the dish should be ready to go. The buttery pine nuts pair well with the sardines. We use fresh sardines here, but canned will work just perfectly, too. **SERVES 4**

PREP TIME: 10 minutes
COOK TIME: 25 minutes

12 ounces spaghetti

3 tablespoons extra-virgin olive oil

4 to 6 fresh sardines, butterflied and boned

Kosher salt

Freshly ground black pepper

1 large red bell pepper, cut into thin strips

1 large shallot, coarsely chopped

¼ cup pine nuts

3 garlic cloves, minced

2 tablespoons unsalted butter

Juice of ½ lemon

2 tablespoons coarsely chopped fresh flat-leaf parsley

1. Bring a large pot of water to a boil over medium-high heat. Add the pasta and cook according to package instructions until tender, about 10 minutes. Reserve 1 cup of pasta water, then drain and set aside.

2. Meanwhile, in a wok or deep sauté pan, heat the olive oil over medium heat. When shimmery wavy lines run through the oil, add the sardines and sear for 6 minutes, flipping them over halfway through. Season with salt and pepper.

3. Using a slotted spoon, transfer the sardines to a plate. Return the pan to medium heat.

4. Add the red bell pepper and shallot and sauté until soft, about 7 minutes. Add the pine nuts, garlic, and butter and sauté until the butter melts and browns slightly.

5. Return the sardines to the pan and fold in gently, breaking them up into smaller chunks and flakes. ❯

6. Transfer the pasta back to the stockpot. Toss in the sardine mixture and drizzle in some of the pasta water to loosen the sauce, if needed.

7. Add the lemon juice and parsley, tossing to coat, and serve.

VARIATION 1 **TUNA WITH PASTA, PINE NUTS, AND RED PEPPER:** Use canned tuna packed in oil instead of sardines and add a generous pinch of red pepper flakes.

VARIATION 2 **SARDINES WITH PASTA AND CAPERS:** Add lemon zest and capers to the sardines when folding them in. The more you can add bright bursts of flavor to this dish, the tastier it will be!

SARDINE CEVICHE

Ceviche originates from Peru. The dish isn't cooked over heat, but rather the acid in the citrus juices "cook" the fish. It's the perfect choice for a hot summer night when you can't bear to turn on the oven or stove. I've also served it in a chilled bowl surrounded with toasted tortilla chips for a party appetizer. **SERVES 4**

PREP TIME: 10 minutes, plus 1 hour to cure

2 to 4 fresh sardine fillets, filleted and boned, then thinly sliced across the grain

1 large red grapefruit, peel and pith removed and segmented

1 lemon, peel and pith removed and segmented

¼ cup extra-virgin olive oil

2 tablespoons finely chopped red onion

Juice of 2 limes

Pinch red pepper flakes

½ teaspoon kosher salt

2 tablespoons chopped fresh cilantro, for garnish

Tortilla chips or endive spears, for serving

1. In a small bowl, fold together the sardines, grapefruit, lemon, olive oil, onion, lime juice, red pepper flakes, and salt.

2. Cover and refrigerate for 1 hour, or until you are ready to serve.

3. Fold in the cilantro just before serving. Serve with tortilla chips or endive spears.

VARIATION 1 PRECOOKED SARDINE CEVICHE: You can certainly use canned sardines for this recipe. Drain the sardines from the can (packed either in water or oil—doesn't matter), and break the fish up gently with a fork before folding it into the ceviche ingredients. Because the canned sardines are already cooked, there is no need to cure the fish in the citrus juices.

VARIATION 2 MACKEREL CEVICHE: Substitute mackerel if fresh sardines are not available.

OIL-PACKED SARDINES WITH SMASHED POTATOES

We call this a pantry salad in my house. I like to have these ingredients on hand so it's easy to whip up a satisfying salad without much effort. Select the smallest potatoes you can find and pick the best quality sardines packed in olive oil. By keeping only the highest quality staples in your pantry, just a few ingredients can become a great dish. **SERVES 6**

PREP TIME: 10 minutes
COOK TIME: 20 minutes

1 pound baby Yukon gold potatoes

¼ cup kosher salt, divided

1 (4.5-ounce) can oil-packed sardines, oil drained and reserved

2 tablespoons extra-virgin olive oil

2 teaspoons freshly squeezed lemon juice

1 teaspoon whole-grain mustard

2 celery stalks, cut into ¼-inch-thick slices on the bias

1 scallion, thinly sliced (white and green parts)

¼ cup chopped fresh flat-leaf parsley

Freshly ground black pepper

1. In a large saucepan, cover the potatoes by about 1 inch of water and add 3½ tablespoons of salt. Bring the water to a boil over high heat, then lower the heat and simmer for about 15 minutes, until tender. Drain and set aside.

2. Meanwhile, use a fork to gently break up the sardines into chunks and set aside.

3. In a wide shallow bowl, whisk together the olive oil, lemon juice, and mustard, then add the celery, sardines, scallion, and parsley. Add the remaining ½ tablespoon of salt and season with pepper.

4. When the potatoes are cool enough to handle, place them on a cutting board. Use a small plate or saucer to gently flatten them, repeating the process until all the potatoes have been flattened.

5. Gently fold the potatoes into the sardine mixture. It's okay if the potatoes break up slightly or if the fish flakes even more. Drizzle with about 2 teaspoons of the reserved sardine oil and serve warm or at room temperature.

VARIATION 1 OIL-PACKED FISH WITH SMASHED POTATOES: You can substitute the sardines with any canned fish (whitefish, trout, salmon, tuna). Just be sure they are packed in oil, as this adds a lot of flavor to the dish.

VARIATION 2 OIL-PACKED SARDINES AND OLIVE SALAD: Add ¼ cup of pitted olives to the salad. Olives and sardines go great together! Bulk up the salad by tossing in 2 cups of shredded radicchio or Belgian endive.

Steamed Whole Mackerel with Sizzling Ginger Oil, page 60

CHAPTER 4

MACKEREL

A relative to tuna, mackerel is a beautiful fish in its own right. Its skin is a luminous iridescent striped or spotty pattern, depending on the type, and its meat is rich and oily. When cooked, mackerel has a rich and fishy flavor with white flaky meat.

Fresh mackerel is a wonder fish: It's inexpensive and packed with omega-3 fatty acids and other important nutrients. Like most types of fish, it is best when eaten fresh, preferably the same day it was caught (its oily nature causes it to develop a fishy flavor fast). If that's not possible, frozen fillets are great, as are the countless recipes available that use canned or smoked mackerel.

As far as sustainability goes, mackerel is quite high on the sustainable scale, with line-caught Atlantic mackerel being the most sustainable. Mackerel can be bony, so I encourage you to use tweezers or needle-nose pliers to remove any pin bones.

STEAMED WHOLE MACKEREL WITH SIZZLING GINGER OIL

Growing up in a Chinese American family, I enjoyed many multicourse banquet dinners in Chinese restaurants. There was always the fish course: a fresh fish steamed whole, smothered with scallions, ginger, and a sizzling oil that was poured over it right before it hit the table. It was the highlight of the meal for my brother and me. We would spoon tender flakes of the fish and the savory-sweet sauce over a bowl of steamed rice and declare it the best course of the entire banquet. I know this recipe seems complicated, but trust me—it's worth the effort. **SERVES 4 TO 6**

PREP TIME: 15 minutes
COOK TIME: 20 minutes

FOR THE FISH

1 (2-pound) whole mackerel, head on

½ cup kosher salt, for cleaning

Freshly ground white pepper

3 to 4 scallions, cut into 3-inch pieces (white and green parts)

½ bunch cilantro

Kosher salt

1 (4-inch) piece fresh ginger, peeled and thinly sliced

2 tablespoons Shaoxing rice wine or dry sherry ❯

1. To make the fish, clean it by rubbing it inside and out with the kosher salt. Rinse the fish and pat dry with paper towels. Season the fish inside and out with salt and pepper.

2. In a steamer basket or on a plate, make a bed using half of each the scallions, cilantro, and ginger. Place the fish on top and stuff the remaining half of each inside the fish. Pour the wine over the fish.

3. Pour 2 inches of water into a wide skillet and bring to a boil over medium heat. Place the steamer basket or plate in the pan and cover. Steam the fish for 15 minutes (adding 2 minutes for every ½ pound beyond 2 pounds), or until a fork inserted near the head flakes the flesh. If the flesh still sticks together, steam for 2 more minutes.

4. To make the sauce, while the fish is steaming, warm the soy sauce, sesame oil, and sugar in a small pan over low heat. Set aside.

FOR THE SAUCE

2 tablespoons light
soy sauce

1 tablespoon sesame oil

2 teaspoons sugar

**FOR THE SIZZLING
GINGER OIL**

3 tablespoons vegetable oil

2 tablespoons
julienned peeled fresh
ginger, divided

2 scallions, thinly sliced on
the bias, divided (white
and green parts)

5. Once the fish is cooked, transfer to a clean platter. Discard the cooking liquid and aromatics from the steaming plate. Pour the warm sauce over the fish. Tent with aluminum foil to keep it warm.

6. To make the sizzling ginger oil, in small saucepan, heat the vegetable oil over medium heat. Just before it starts to smoke, add half the ginger and half the scallions and fry for 10 seconds. Pour the sizzling oil over the fish.

7. Garnish with the remaining half of scallions and ginger and serve immediately.

VARIATION 1 SPICY STEAMED MACKEREL: Slice some small Thai chiles to sizzle in the ginger oil, introducing more heat to the dish. Increase the fragrance of the dish by adding 2 tablespoons of chopped Thai basil.

VARIATION 2 STEAMED WHITEFISH OR CLAMS WITH SIZZLING GINGER OIL: Truth be told, any whole, flaky whitefish would work well with this preparation. I've even had success steaming clams in this manner. The sizzling ginger oil is fantastic with clams!

BROILED MACKEREL WITH LEMON BEURRE BLANC SAUCE

Beurre blanc is a tangy, velvety sauce made from reduced wine and shallots that is whisked with an alarming amount of butter. It's a classic French sauce that is perfect for any seafood. I picked up on its importance when our chef instructor taught us how to make it on two occasions, stressing how miserably we all failed at it the first time. The secret that no one tells you is to reduce the liquid until it is practically dry in the pan before whisking in the butter. **SERVES 4**

PREP TIME: 10 minutes
COOK TIME: 15 minutes

2 (6- to 8-ounce) mackerel fillets

1 tablespoon extra-virgin olive oil

Kosher salt

Freshly ground black pepper

1 cup dry white wine (such as Sauvignon blanc)

1 shallot, finely chopped

Zest and juice of 1 lemon

6 tablespoons (¾ stick) unsalted butter, cold and cubed

½ cup sliced toasted almonds, for garnish

3 tablespoons chopped fresh mint leaves, for garnish

1. Preheat the oven to 425°F or turn on the broiler.

2. Line a baking sheet with aluminum foil and place the mackerel fillets side by side on it. Drizzle with the olive oil and season with salt and pepper.

3. Roast or broil for 8 minutes, until the fish feels firm and has a slightly opaque look. Transfer to a warm platter and tent with foil.

4. In a nonstick skillet over medium-high heat, sauté the wine, shallot, lemon zest, and lemon juice until it reduces and is almost dry, 5 to 7 minutes.

5. Begin to add the cubes of butter, a few at a time, while whisking constantly. Be sure that the butter has completely melted before adding more. This ensures that the sauce is velvety and slightly foamy. Lightly season with salt and pepper.

6. Pour the beurre blanc over the mackerel and garnish with the almonds and mint. Serve hot.

VARIATION 1 BROILED MACKEREL WITH PINEAPPLE BEURRE BLANC SAUCE: Make the mackerel a bit tropical by using pineapple juice instead of lemon juice in the sauce. Garnish the fish with diced pineapple, macadamia nuts, and mint.

VARIATION 2 BROILED FISH WITH BEURRE BLANC SAUCE: You can substitute salmon, catfish, tilapia, or trout to serve with a beurre blanc sauce.

ROASTED MACKEREL WITH GARLIC AND PAPRIKA BREAD CRUMBS

I get asked a lot of cooking questions by friends and family. But the one I hear the most is about how to cook and eat fish at home, since it's healthier. That's usually followed by a request that it be quick and easy and tasty. Oh, and it can't be boring. When I get cornered, I usually suggest this recipe. It checks all of those boxes. **SERVES 4**

PREP TIME: 15 minutes
COOK TIME: 10 minutes

¼ cup plus 1 teaspoon extra-virgin olive oil, divided

4 mackerel fillets (1½ pound), skin on

Kosher salt

Freshly ground black pepper

Zest and juice of 1 lemon, divided

1 cup panko bread crumbs

2 tablespoons coarsely chopped fresh flat-leaf parsley

3 small garlic cloves, minced

1 teaspoon smoked paprika

1. Preheat the oven to 400°F. Rub 1 teaspoon of olive oil over the inside of a 9-by-13-inch baking dish.

2. Place the mackerel fillets, skin-side down, in a single layer in the prepared baking dish. Drizzle with 2 tablespoons of olive oil and season with salt and pepper. Drizzle 2 teaspoons of lemon juice over the fish and reserve the rest. Roast for 8 minutes.

3. While the fish is roasting, in a nonstick skillet over medium heat, combine the remaining 2 tablespoons of olive oil, the lemon zest, bread crumbs, parsley, garlic, and paprika and cook, stirring occasionally, until the garlic is fragrant and the bread crumbs are golden and toasty. Season with salt and pepper.

4. Remove the fish from the oven and top with the bread crumb mixture. Drizzle the remaining lemon juice over the fish and serve immediately.

VARIATION 1 ROASTED MACKEREL WITH CORIANDER BREAD CRUMBS: You can switch out the aromatics and herbs to create new flavor combinations, like orange zest, fresh mint, and ground coriander.

VARIATION 2 ALMOND-CRUSTED MACKEREL: Use almond meal instead of the bread crumbs and mint instead of the parsley. Fresh mint can balance the rich oils from both the fish and nuts.

MACKEREL MEUNIÈRE

Julia Child's first meal in Paris was sole meunière. It was drenched in butter and so began her love affair with French cooking, and her destiny. "Meunière" translates to the "miller's wife"—she has access to as much flour as she wants, of course. This is a rustic, informal dish made of filleted fish dredged in flour and panfried with lots of butter and lemon. **SERVES 4**

PREP TIME: 10 minutes
COOK TIME: 15 minutes

4 mackerel fillets (1½ pound), skin and pin bones removed

Kosher salt

Freshly ground black pepper

⅔ cup all-purpose flour

2 tablespoons vegetable oil or canola oil

8 tablespoons (1 stick) unsalted butter, cut into ½-inch cubes, divided

Juice of ½ lemon

2 tablespoons coarsely chopped fresh flat-leaf parsley

Lemon wedges, for garnish

1. Arrange the mackerel on a plate and season generously on both sides with salt and pepper. Pour the flour into a wide shallow dish and dredge the fish generously on both sides.

2. In a large nonstick skillet, heat the oil over medium-high heat. When shimmery wavy lines run through the oil, add 3 tablespoons of butter and quickly swirl to combine it with the oil. Add the fish and cook for 6 minutes, flipping over halfway through, until both sides are golden brown.

3. Transfer the fish to plates and tent with aluminum foil.

4. To prepare the sauce, pour off the oil from cooking the fish and wipe the pan clean. Return the pan to medium-high heat and add the remaining 5 tablespoons of butter and cook until the milk solids begin to brown, 3 to 4 minutes. Remove from the heat and gently stir in the lemon juice and parsley. Season with salt and pepper and spoon the sauce over the fish.

5. Garnish with lemon wedges and serve.

VARIATION 1 **MACKEREL MEUNIÈRE WITH CAPERS:** Though not traditional, adding 1 teaspoon of chopped capers wakes up the dish with bursts of brininess.

VARIATION 1 **ASIAN-STYLE MACKEREL MEUNIÈRE:** For an Asian twist, mix the butter with 2 minced garlic cloves, a finely chopped scallion, and 2 teaspoons of soy sauce.

MACKEREL PIPERADE

Piperade is a rustic Basque stew made of peppers, onions, and tomatoes. The colors of the vegetables represent the colors on the Basque flag: white, red, and green. Traditionally, cod is simmered in the piperade but mackerel is a great alternative, as it goes really well with olives and peppers. **SERVES 4**

PREP TIME: 10 minutes
COOK TIME: 25 minutes

4 mackerel fillets
(1½ pound), skin and pin
bones removed

Kosher salt

Freshly ground
black pepper

6 tablespoons extra-virgin
olive oil, divided, plus more
for garnish

1 medium white onion, cut
into ½-inch strips

1 red bell pepper, cut into
½-inch strips

1 green bell pepper, cut
into ½-inch strips

2 garlic cloves, minced

1 tablespoon
smoked paprika

Pinch cayenne pepper

1 (14-ounce) can
fire-roasted diced
tomatoes, with their juices

1 cup halved pitted
green olives

2 tablespoons coarsely
chopped fresh flat-leaf
parsley, for garnish

1. Season the mackerel fillets with salt and pepper and drizzle 2 tablespoons of olive oil over the fish. Set aside on a plate.

2. In a large wide sauté pan or skillet, heat the remaining 4 tablespoons olive oil over medium-high heat. Add the onion and red and green bell peppers and cook until tender, about 7 minutes. Season with salt and pepper.

3. Add the garlic, paprika, and cayenne and sauté for 1 minute, until the garlic is fragrant.

4. Add the tomatoes and their juices and stir gently to combine. Season with salt and pepper and add the olives. Lower the heat to medium and simmer for 5 minutes.

5. Place the mackerel in the sauce and simmer, covered, for 10 minutes.

6. Serve hot, garnished with the parsley and a drizzle of olive oil.

VARIATION 1 PIPERADE BREAKFAST: You can make a very hearty breakfast dish here by simmering a couple of cracked eggs in the piperade and stirring in some flaked smoked mackerel toward the end.

VARIATION 2 MACKEREL PIPERADE WITH CHORIZO: Make a heartier stew by adding diced Spanish chorizo to the vegetables as they are being sautéed.

MISO-LACQUERED MACKEREL WITH CRISPY RICE CAKES

Adding a glazed sauce to fish and broiling it for a few moments creates a shiny, caramelized coating with a lacquer-like finish. It's dramatic and delicious. I make the extra effort to serve the fish with crispy rice cakes because the flavors and textures are perfect together. **SERVES 4**

PREP TIME: 20 minutes
COOK TIME: 40 minutes

FOR THE RICE CAKES

1 cup short-grain sushi rice

1 tablespoon seasoned rice vinegar

1 teaspoon kosher salt

2 tablespoons vegetable oil

FOR THE MACKEREL

3 tablespoons vegetable oil, divided

2 tablespoons soy sauce

2 tablespoons yellow miso

1 tablespoon toasted sesame oil

1 tablespoon honey

4 mackerel fillets (1 pound), skin on and pin bones removed

4 lemon wedges or slices, for garnish

2 scallions, thinly sliced on the bias, for garnish (white and green parts)

1. Preheat the oven to 400°F. Line a baking sheet with aluminum foil.

2. To make the rice cakes, cook the rice according to the package instructions, about 20 minutes. While the rice is cooking, stir together the vinegar and salt. Set aside.

3. When the rice is done, transfer it to a mixing bowl and gently fluff with a kitchen spoon, letting it cool. Add the vinegar mixture and stir once more. Divide the rice into four equal balls.

4. With wet hands, shape the balls into tightly compacted 1-inch-thick patties and wrap each patty tightly with plastic wrap.

5. In a nonstick skillet, heat the vegetable oil over medium heat. When shimmery wavy lines run through the oil, unwrap the patties and carefully place them in the skillet.

6. Fry until the undersides are golden brown and crispy, about 5 minutes. Flip the rice cakes over and fry on the other side until golden and crispy, about 4 minutes. Transfer the rice cakes to plates and keep warm. ❯

7. To make the mackerel, in a small bowl, whisk 2 tablespoons of the vegetable oil, soy sauce, miso, sesame oil, and honey together until it forms a thick paste.

8. Spread the remaining 1 tablespoon of oil over the prepared baking sheet. Place the fish on the baking sheet and brush the marinade over the tops of the fish. Roast for 8 minutes. Remove from the oven and brush again with more marinade.

9. Adjust the oven to broil on high and broil for 1 to 2 minutes, or until the tops of the fillets become slightly caramelized. Remove from the broiler and transfer to the plates with the rice cakes.

10. Garnish with the lemon and scallions and serve immediately.

VARIATION 1 SPICY MISO-LACQUERED MACKEREL WITH CRISPY RICE CAKES: Blend some chopped garlic, ginger, and shallots in to the miso marinade for a super spicy lacquer.

VARIATION 2 MISO-LACQUERED MACKEREL WITH CRISPY FURIKAKE RICE CAKES: Fold a couple of tablespoons of furikake into the rice before shaping it into cakes.

SMOKED MACKEREL PINTXOS

Pintxos (pronounces "PEEN-choes") are the Basque version of Spanish tapas. They're usually offered at the bar and plated and served by the bartender. They're usually very protein-heavy, so one or two per drink is all you need. When I was in San Sebastián, I quickly learned that a bar with crumpled up cocktail napkins littered across the floor was usually a good indicator of delicious pintxos. **SERVES 4 TO 6**

PREP TIME: 20 minutes
COOK TIME: 25 minutes

1 medium potato, peeled and cut into 1-inch chunks

¼ cup kosher salt, divided

1 baguette, cut into 12 (¼-inch-thick) slices on the bias

¼ cup extra-virgin olive oil, divided

Freshly ground black pepper

4 ounces Spanish chorizo, casing removed and finely chopped

1 small shallot, finely chopped

2 tablespoons unsalted butter

2 smoked mackerel fillets (1 pound), broken up into chunks

2 tablespoons coarsely chopped fresh flat-leaf parsley, divided

1 (4-ounce) jar pimento strips, drained

1. Preheat the oven to 400°F.

2. In a small saucepan, cover the potatoes with water and add 3 tablespoons of kosher salt. Bring to a boil over medium-high heat, then lower the heat to medium-low and simmer for 8 to 10 minutes, until tender. Drain and set aside in a mixing bowl.

3. On a baking sheet, arrange the baguette slices in a single layer and brush the tops lightly with 2 tablespoons of olive oil. Season with ½ tablespoon of salt and pepper and toast for 10 minutes. Remove from the oven and set aside to cool.

4. In a nonstick skillet, heat the remaining 2 tablespoons of olive oil over medium heat. When shimmery wavy lines run through the oil add the chorizo and shallot and sauté until the shallot is soft and translucent, about 4 minutes. Season with the remaining ½ tablespoon of salt and pepper. Add the chorizo mixture to the potato.

5. Return the skillet to medium heat and melt the butter. Add the smoked mackerel, breaking up the fish into smaller flakes and swirling the butter to coat it. Remove from the heat and add to the potato. ❯

6. With a potato masher, mash the potato mixture together until combined and smooth. Fold in 1 tablespoon of parsley and season with salt and pepper.

7. To serve, divide and spread the potato mixture evenly among the toasted baguette and top with a few pimento strips. Sprinkle the remaining 1 tablespoon of parsley over the pintxos and transfer to a platter. Serve warm or at room temperature.

VARIATION 1 **CANNED MACKEREL PINTXOS:** If smoked mackerel isn't available, use canned mackerel packed in olive oil and add a pinch or two of smoked paprika.

VARIATION 2 **SMOKED MACKEREL-STUFFED SWEET PEPPERS:** Stuff the potato and mackerel mixture into fire-roasted mini sweet peppers. You can find fresh mini sweet peppers in the produce area of your supermarket and fire-roast them, or find a jar of roasted peppers in the aisles where the pickles and olives are located.

HERB-STUFFED ROASTED MACKEREL WITH CAULIFLOWER AND ROASTED TOMATOES

This recipe makes a stunning presentation, especially on a bed of greens. Preheating the skillet before roasting is an important step—it helps the cooking process go much faster! **SERVES 4**

PREP TIME: 15 minutes
COOK TIME: 20 minutes

2 (2-pound) whole mackerel, skin and pin bones removed and butterflied

6 tablespoons extra-virgin olive oil, divided

Kosher salt

Freshly ground black pepper

2 lemons, thinly sliced, divided

½ bunch dill

½ bunch flat-leaf parsley leaves

½ bunch oregano

½ head cauliflower, cut into bite-size florets

3 cups grape tomatoes

½ medium red onion, unpeeled and cut into ½-inch slices

3 tablespoons vegetable oil

2 large handfuls baby arugula, spinach, or kale

1. Preheat the oven to 425°F. Place a 12-inch cast iron skillet in the oven to preheat for at least 15 minutes.

2. Open a mackerel like a book and place it flat, skin-side down. Drizzle with 2 tablespoons of olive oil and season with salt and pepper. Add 3 lemon slices and half the dill, parsley, and oregano and fold the mackerel over to close. Set aside and repeat the process with the remaining mackerel.

3. Using a sharp knife, score three to four diagonal cuts across the top of each fish, cutting about ¼-inch deep. Halve four lemon slices to create half-moons and stuff them into the scores.

4. Rub 2 tablespoons of olive oil over both sides of the fish and season with salt and pepper.

5. In a medium bowl, toss the cauliflower, tomatoes, and red onion together with the remaining 2 tablespoons of olive oil and season with salt and pepper.

6. Remove the pan from the oven and place on a heat-proof surface. Add the vegetable oil and swirl to coat the pan. When shimmery wavy lines run through the oil, place the mackerel side by side in the pan and toss the vegetables around it, being careful as the hot pan may start sizzling right away. ❯

7. Return the pan to the oven and roast for 20 minutes, or until the vegetables have roasted and caramelized slightly.

8. Create a bed of the arugula on a platter and place the fish on top. Arrange the roasted vegetables around the fish and serve hot.

VARIATION 1 ASIAN-STYLE ROASTED MACKEREL AND VEGETABLES: Change up the dish for a more Asian-flavored recipe by using limes, scallions, ginger, cilantro, and garlic. You can sauté some baby bok choy and add that to the greens as well.

VARIATION 2 ROASTED MACKEREL WITH TAPENADE: Simplify, but don't compromise on flavor. Roast multicolored carrots and cauliflower with chunks of red onion. Stuff the mackerel with lemon and parsley and spread 1 tablespoon of tapenade down each side of the fish before folding it up.

Tilapia Tacos with Creamy Cabbage Slaw, page 78

CHAPTER 5

TILAPIA

Tilapia is an inexpensive freshwater fish that is mild in flavor, with a firm and flaky texture. It's a great place to start if you are unfamiliar with cooking fish at home. This tender whitefish goes well with so many different flavor profiles and is so widely available in supermarkets across the country in both fresh and frozen options, it really should be considered the "chicken of the sea." Because it comes from fresh water, tilapia doesn't taste or smell very "fishy."

The fish is nutrient-dense, a great source of protein, and is extremely low in fat. One 4-ounce serving provides 26 grams of protein and just 3 grams of fat. Wild-caught tilapia is very hard to find; however, sustainably farm-raised tilapia is available from countries such as the United States, Canada, the Netherlands, Ecuador, and Peru.

CLASSIC FISH AND CHIPS

You can't walk down a commercial street in London without discovering small hole-in-the-wall fish and chip joints called "chippies." If you aren't sure what to order, simply pay attention to the person before you. Most likely they're a local and you won't be steered wrong. This recipe is my variation of classic British fish and chips. **SERVES 4**

PREP TIME: 30 minutes
COOK TIME: 30 minutes

3 large russet potatoes, peeled and cut into 1-by-1½-inch strips

6 cups vegetable oil, for frying

¾ cup all-purpose flour, divided

¼ cup rice flour

¼ cup cornstarch

1 teaspoon baking powder

½ teaspoon cayenne pepper

Kosher salt

Freshly ground black pepper

⅓ cup beer (such as Newcastle Brown Ale, but any beer will do)

⅓ cup sparkling water

4 (4- to 5-ounce) tilapia fillets, each cut into 3 pieces and blotted dry

Malt vinegar, for serving

Lemon wedges, for serving

1. To prepare the chips, in a bowl of cold water, soak the potatoes for up to 30 minutes. Drain and blot dry.

2. In a 3-quart Dutch oven or wide saucepan, heat the oil over medium-high heat to 350°F. Test the oil by dropping a spoonful of batter into it. If the batter begins to fry immediately and float, the oil is ready for frying.

3. While the oil is heating, in a bowl, whisk together ¼ cup of flour, the rice flour, cornstarch, baking powder, and cayenne. Season with a pinch of salt and pepper. Whisk in the beer and sparkling water until a light, foamy batter develops and the mixture is smooth.

4. Preheat the oven to 300°F.

5. When the oil is ready, using a wire skimmer, gently lower the chips, working in batches, into the pot. Fry for 7 to 8 minutes, until golden and cooked through. Remove the chips from the oil and transfer to a wire rack set over a baking sheet to drain.

6. Turn off the stove and place the chips in the oven to keep them warm.

7. Season both sides of the fish with salt and pepper. On a wide plate, add the remaining ½ cup of flour and dredge a piece of fish in the flour to evenly coat. Shake off the excess and dip the fish into the batter, making sure the batter completely coats the fish. Repeat the process with the remaining fillets.

8. Turn the heat back on and bring the oil temperature to 375°F. Using a pair of tongs, lift the fish from the batter and gently lower it into the oil. Cook in batches, up to four pieces of fish at time. Fry for 5 to 6 minutes, or until golden brown and crispy. Using a wire skimmer or slotted spoon, lift the fish out of the oil and place on a plate lined with paper towels. Keep warm in the oven.

9. To serve, arrange the fish and chips on a platter. Drizzle malt vinegar over the fish and garnish with lemon wedges. Serve hot.

VARIATION 1 **CARIBBEAN FISH AND CHIPS:** Give your fish and chips a Caribbean twist by adding a shot of rum to the batter and 1/2 cup of shredded coconut. Make the chips from sweet potatoes, plantains, sliced chiles, and onion rings and squeeze lime juice to serve instead of malt vinegar.

VARIATION 2 **FISH AND PEAS:** Bright green smashed peas or "mushy peas" lend some color and green to the dish and would be perfectly appropriate to add to your plate. Cook 2 cups of frozen peas with 1/2 cup of water and a pinch of salt. Drain and add 2 tablespoons of unsalted butter and chopped mint. Mash and serve in spoonfuls with the fish.

TILAPIA TACOS WITH CREAMY CABBAGE SLAW

Since Taco Tuesday is actually a thing, why not make it Tilapia Taco Tuesday? Tilapia is an excellent choice for fish tacos because it's delicate enough that it doesn't overwhelm the other ingredients, but it's also sturdy enough to maintain its structure. **SERVES 4 (2 TACOS EACH)**

PREP TIME: 10 minutes
COOK TIME: 20 minutes

FOR THE CABBAGE SLAW

½ head green cabbage, finely shredded

½ small red onion, cut into ¼-inch dice

¼ cup loosely packed fresh cilantro leaves

1 small jalapeño, seeded and minced

Kosher salt

Freshly ground black pepper

2 tablespoons sour cream or Mexican crema

1 tablespoon freshly squeezed lime juice ❯

1. To make the cabbage slaw, in a small bowl, toss together the cabbage, onion, cilantro, and jalapeño. Season with salt and pepper. Toss with the sour cream and lime juice and keep covered in the refrigerator.

2. To make the tacos, heat a cast iron skillet over medium-high heat. While the pan is heating, season both sides of the fish with the cumin, chile powder, salt, and pepper.

3. Add the oil to the pan. When the oil reaches its smoke point, add the fish and sear on each side for 4 minutes, flipping once. Transfer the fillets to a clean plate and tent with aluminum foil.

4. Wipe out the pan with dry paper towels and return it to medium-high heat. Toast the tortillas, two at a time, for 1 minute each, flipping halfway through.

FOR THE TACOS

2 tilapia fillets
(1½ pound), each cut
into 4 equal pieces

1 teaspoon ground cumin

½ teaspoon chile powder

Kosher salt

Freshly ground
black pepper

3 tablespoons vegetable oil

16 (6-inch) corn tortillas

2 limes, quartered,
for garnish

5. To assemble, break the fillets into small chunks and arrange on top of eight double stacks of tortillas. Lightly season each taco with salt and pepper and a squeeze of juice from the limes. Top with the cabbage slaw. Serve immediately.

VARIATION 1 SHRIMP TACOS WITH CREAMY CABBAGE SLAW: Shrimp tacos are just as delicious and cook up even faster than tilapia!

VARIATION 2 TILAPIA TACOS WITH AVOCADO AND BLACK BEANS: Round out the tacos and make them more robust by slipping in slices of avocado for a creamy element and adding some cooked black beans and thinly sliced radishes.

ROASTED TILAPIA WITH ORZO AND TOMATOES

This is a really light dish, perfect for days when you don't want to have something heavy but still want something delicious and satisfying. Orzo is a short, flat rice-shaped pasta that is usually found in soups. It works great as a short pasta in place of rice pilaf with tomatoes and oregano.

SERVES 4

PREP TIME: 15 minutes
COOK TIME: 15 minutes

1 lemon, zested and cut into ¼-inch slices

4 tilapia fillets (1½ pound)

¼ cup extra-virgin olive oil, divided

Kosher salt

Freshly ground black pepper

2 tablespoons coarsely chopped fresh oregano leaves, divided

1 shallot, coarsely chopped

2 cups halved grape tomatoes

2 cups cooked orzo

1 tablespoon coarsely chopped fresh flat-leaf parsley

2 tablespoons crumbled feta cheese, for garnish (optional)

1. Preheat the oven to 400°F. Line a baking sheet with aluminum foil or parchment paper.

2. Arrange the lemon slices in a single layer on the prepared baking sheet and place the tilapia across the lemon slices.

3. Drizzle with 2 tablespoons of olive oil and season with salt and pepper. Rub the oil and seasonings all over both sides of the fish and sprinkle 1 tablespoon of oregano over the fish. Roast for 10 to 15 minutes, or until the fish flakes with a fork.

4. While the fish is roasting, in a sauté pan or skillet, heat the remaining 2 tablespoons of olive oil over medium-high heat. When shimmery wavy lines run through the oil, add the shallot and sauté until soft and translucent, about 4 minutes, then add the tomatoes. Cook for 5 minutes, or until the tomatoes begin to soften and break down.

5. Remove the pan from the heat and stir in the cooked orzo, lemon zest, parsley, and the remaining 1 tablespoon of oregano. Lightly season with salt and pepper and transfer to a serving platter.

6. Carefully transfer each fillet to the a bed of the orzo mixture. Garnish with the feta cheese (if using) and serve hot.

VARIATION 1 ROASTED TILAPIA WITH PASTA SALAD:
To bulk up the orzo and tomatoes, you can make a pasta salad by adding sliced olives or capers and a handful of toasted pine nuts. Substitute farfalle for the orzo.

VARIATION 2 ROASTED TILAPIA WITH ORZO AND PEAS:
Substitute chopped fresh mint leaves for the oregano and 1 cup of green peas for the tomatoes for a lighter, fresher twist on this dish.

TILAPIA IN MUSTARD SAUCE

After coming home from a long day at work, you can push away the "what's for dinner" panic by pulling out one of my favorite go-to recipes. Frozen tilapia can thaw quickly, and we always have multiple jars of mustard in the back of our refrigerator. In the time it takes to pull this together, make a quick salad and open a bottle of wine. **SERVES 4**

PREP TIME: 10 minutes
COOK TIME: 15 minutes

4 (6-ounce) tilapia fillets

Kosher salt

Freshly ground
black pepper

2 tablespoons extra-virgin
olive oil

1 cup sour cream

2 tablespoons
Dijon mustard

2 teaspoons
whole-grain mustard

1 small shallot, minced

1 teaspoon coarsely
chopped capers

1. Preheat the oven to 400°F. Line a baking sheet with parchment paper or aluminum foil.

2. Arrange the fish on the prepared baking sheet and season on both sides with salt and pepper. Rub the olive oil all over the fish. Set aside.

3. In a small bowl, stir together the sour cream, Dijon mustard, and whole-grain mustard. Add the shallot and capers, season with salt and pepper, and mix well. Spread the sauce over the fish, completely covering each fillet.

4. Roast for 12 minutes. Remove from the oven and transfer to plates. Serve immediately.

VARIATION 1 TILAPIA IN WHITE WINE MUSTARD SAUCE:
Use heavy cream instead of sour cream and add a splash of white wine to the mustard. The sauce comes out a little thinner, but the wine brings out a sweetness in the fish. Herbs like tarragon or chervil help bring the whole dish together with their delicate licorice flavor.

VARIATION 2 TILAPIA IN MUSTARD SAUCE WITH BACON:
Bacon makes everything better, including this dish! Chop up 2 or 3 bacon slices and cook until the bacon bits are brown and crispy. Add the bacon to the mustard sauce.

THAI-SPICED TILAPIA IN GREEN CURRY

This is one of those recipes where people will have one whiff and want to know what you're cooking and when it will be ready. The perfume of coconut milk and the curry spices can travel down the hall and into the street, so make more of it than you actually need. **SERVES 4**

PREP TIME: 15 minutes
COOK TIME: 35 minutes

2 tablespoons coconut oil

1 large shallot,
finely chopped

2½ tablespoons Thai green
curry paste

1 (15-ounce) can
coconut milk

¼ cup low-sodium
vegetable stock

2 teaspoons fish sauce

Kosher salt

Freshly ground
black pepper

4 tilapia fillets (1½ pound)

2 scallions, thinly sliced,
for garnish (white and
green parts)

2 tablespoons shredded
Thai basil, for garnish
(about 8 leaves)

1 lime, cut into wedges,
for garnish

Cooked rice, for serving

1. Preheat the oven to 350°F.

2. Heat a large oven-safe skillet over medium-high heat. Add the coconut oil and swirl to coat the pan. When the oil has melted, add the shallot and sauté for about 4 minutes, until it is soft and translucent.

3. Add the green curry paste and stir to combine. Lower the heat to medium-low and add the coconut milk. Simmer for 5 minutes, stirring occasionally.

4. Stir in the vegetable stock and fish sauce and lightly season with salt and pepper. Continue to simmer for 2 minutes.

5. Season both sides of the tilapia with salt and pepper and place in the curry sauce. Transfer the pan to the oven. Bake, uncovered, for 25 minutes, or until the tilapia feels firm and flakes slightly when pushed with a fork.

6. Garnish with the scallions, basil, and lime. Serve immediately with cooked rice.

VARIATION 1 THAI TILAPIA IN RED CURRY: Substitute red or yellow curry paste for a milder curry.

VARIATION 2 COCONUT CURRY TILAPIA: Can't find curry paste? No problem. Use 2 tablespoons of curry powder (any type) for a vibrant yellow curry.

CAJUN TILAPIA PO' BOYS

A traditional Louisiana Po' Boy sandwich can feature fried shrimp, fried oysters, or a slab of fried fish. As a twist, I've slathered Cajun-seasoned mayo over the fish and flash-broiled it to make it lighter and more flavorful.

SERVES 4

PREP TIME: 10 minutes
COOK TIME: 15 minutes

1 teaspoon garlic powder

½ teaspoon chili powder

½ teaspoon dried thyme

½ teaspoon paprika

½ teaspoon onion powder

½ teaspoons kosher salt

¼ teaspoon cayenne pepper

3 tablespoons mayonnaise, divided

2 tilapia fillets (1½ pound)

2 French sandwich rolls, split

2 ripe Roma tomatoes, cut into ¼-inch slices

2 to 3 green leaf lettuce leaves, washed and spun dry

1. Preheat the broiler. Line a baking sheet with aluminum foil and set aside.

2. In a small bowl, mix together the garlic powder, chili powder, thyme, paprika, onion powder, salt, and cayenne pepper. Add 1½ tablespoons of mayonnaise and stir to combine.

3. Spread the spiced mayonnaise over both sides of the fish and place the fish on the prepared baking sheet. Broil the fish for 5 minutes on each side (it's OK if the fish blackens a bit), flipping once. Remove from the broiler and tent with foil.

4. Spread out the rolls under the broiler and toast for a few seconds. Transfer the rolls to plates and spread the remaining 1½ tablespoons of mayonnaise on one side of each roll. Transfer a fillet to each roll and top with the tomatoes and lettuce. Serve hot.

VARIATION 1 CAJUN PO' BOYS WITH SLAW: Add a crunchy slaw to balance the heat from the spice rub. Mix 2 cups of shredded green cabbage, a grated carrot, and chopped parsley with 2 tablespoons of Greek yogurt or mayonnaise, 2 tablespoons of lemon juice, and salt and pepper.

VARIATION 2 STOVETOP PO' BOYS: Skillet-fry the tilapia after you have applied the spice rub and sprinkle some Louisiana Hot Sauce over the fish before serving.

COCONUT-POACHED TILAPIA WITH BOK CHOY AND MUSHROOMS

Gently simmering a delicate protein in a seasoned liquid can infuse bold flavors quickly that taste as though they have been slow-cooking all day long. Use full-fat coconut milk for a more luscious flavor and texture.

SERVES 4

PREP TIME: 15 minutes
COOK TIME: 30 minutes

3 tablespoons coconut oil, divided

2 cups thinly sliced and stemmed shiitake mushrooms

2 Fresno peppers, seeded, deveined, and finely chopped

2 (15-ounce) cans coconut milk

Zest and juice of 1 lime

Kosher salt

Freshly ground black pepper

4 tilapia fillets (1½ pound)

4 baby bok choy bulbs, leaves and stems coarsely chopped

1. Heat a deep skillet over medium-high heat. Add 2 tablespoons of coconut oil and swirl to coat the pan. When the oil has melted, add the mushrooms and sauté for 5 to 7 minutes, until they are golden brown. Transfer to a plate.

2. Add the remaining 1 tablespoon of coconut oil and the peppers and sauté until they are soft and tender, about 4 minutes. Transfer to the plate with the mushrooms.

3. Lower the heat to medium and add the coconut milk, lime zest, and lime juice. Stir to combine and lightly season with salt and pepper. Bring the mixture to a simmer.

4. While simmering, season the tilapia on both sides with salt and pepper. Lower the heat to medium-low and gently slip the fillets into the coconut milk. The fillets should be partially submerged, if not completely covered, in the milk. Let the heat from the milk gently poach the fish for about 8 minutes. Do not let the coconut milk boil.

5. Carefully lift the tilapia from the coconut milk and place in shallow bowls. Cover with aluminum foil. ❯

6. Add the bok choy to the skillet and cook in the coconut milk until tender, about 5 minutes. Add the mushrooms and peppers and stir together until just warmed through.

7. Spoon the sauce over the fish and divide the vegetables evenly among the bowls. Serve hot.

VARIATION 1 COCONUT-POACHED TILAPIA WITH CRISPY RICE: Creamy coconut milk, flaky fish, and tender vegetables. Add another textural element to the dish by serving a sprinkling of crispy rice over the fish. Fry 1 or 2 tablespoons of cooled cooked rice in 2 cups of vegetable oil until the rice puffs and becomes crispy. Transfer to a plate lined with paper towels to drain before garnishing.

VARIATION 2 THAI-SEASONED COCONUT-POACHED TILAPIA: Punch up the Thai flavors by steeping the coconut milk with sliced ginger, a crushed lemongrass stalk, and 1 tablespoon of fish sauce. Adding a tablespoon of curry powder gives the dish color and warmth, which would be perfect to have on a cold, rainy night.

TILAPIA PICCATA

Lemon, butter, and white wine—it's a classic combination for light proteins, such as flaky whitefish, chicken, or veal. My advice is not to skimp on the butter—you might be tempted, but trust me: It helps round out the sharp lemony tartness and brings a rich flavor to the dish. **SERVES 4**

PREP TIME: 10 minutes
COOK TIME: 15 minutes

3 tablespoons unsalted butter, divided

2 tablespoons extra-virgin olive oil

4 tilapia fillets (1½ pound), blotted dry

Kosher salt

Freshly ground black pepper

¾ cup all-purpose flour

½ cup dry white wine (such as Sauvignon blanc)

Juice of ½ lemon

2 teaspoons coarsely chopped rinsed capers

2 tablespoons coarsely chopped fresh flat-leaf parsley, for garnish

1. Heat a large nonstick skillet over medium-high heat and melt 2 tablespoons of butter and the oil together.

2. Season both sides of the fish with salt and pepper. Lightly dredge the fillets in the flour and shake off the excess.

3. When the butter has melted, swirl it to combine with the oil. Place the fillets in the pan and sear for 3 to 4 minutes on each side, or until golden brown and crispy. Transfer the fillets to plates and tent with aluminum foil.

4. Lower the heat to medium and add the wine. Using a wooden spoon, scrape up the bits of browned butter and flour. Stir in the lemon juice and capers, and salt and pepper. Simmer for 2 minutes to reduce the sauce.

5. Remove from the heat and add the remaining 1 tablespoon of butter, swirling until it is melted. Divide the sauce among the plates and garnish each with the parsley. Serve immediately.

VARIATION 1 GLUTEN-FREE TILAPIA PICCATA: For a gluten-free alternative, use almond or hazelnut flour. The nuts will further enhance the nuttiness of the brown butter and offer some added protein to the dish.

VARIATION 2 GREEK-INSPIRED TILAPIA PICCATA: Make it Greek by using pitted chopped kalamata olives instead of capers and fresh oregano instead of parsley.

Chili-Lime Catfish with Charred Corn Salad, page 94

CHAPTER 6

CATFISH

Catfish has taken its position as king of soul food, with its roots going all the way back to colonial times. It remained on the dinner tables in the Southern states through the 1960s, when supply increased enough to make catfish readily available in grocery stores across the country.

Catfish is an extremely versatile whitefish. Its mild flavor can stand up to nearly every flavor profile, from simple fried recipes to spicy stews and everything in between. When shopping for catfish fillets, frozen can be an option over fresh, especially if you have a busy schedule and a late dinner during the week is the norm.

Keep an eye out for US-farmed catfish, such as channel or blue catfish, and avoid any catfish imported from Asian countries. Nutritionally, US-farmed catfish contain 16 grams of protein, 6 grams of fat, and 100 percent of the recommended amount of vitamin B12 per every three ounces.

CATFISH CURRY WITH BASMATI RICE

This comforting fish stew is perfect for a cold night. Catfish is such a mild whitefish it goes perfectly with an Indian curry—the mildness of the fish serves as a terrific backdrop for the rich and spicy curry. If you find the curry to be too spicy, knock it back with some fresh lemon juice. **SERVES 4**

PREP TIME: 20 minutes
COOK TIME: 30 minutes

1½ cups basmati rice

3 tablespoons coconut oil

1 large yellow onion, cut into ¼-inch dice

Kosher salt

Freshly ground black pepper

1 (½-inch) piece fresh ginger, peeled and minced

2 garlic cloves, minced

2 tablespoons tomato paste

1 (15-ounce) can coconut milk

2 tablespoons Madras curry powder

2 cups water

4 (6-ounce) catfish fillets, each cut into 4 pieces

2 tablespoons coarsely chopped fresh cilantro, for garnish

1. In a large bowl, rinse the basmati rice several times, swirling the rice in the water each time to loosen any dust and debris. Cover the rice with fresh water and soak for 15 minutes.

2. While the rice is soaking, heat a large sauté pan or skillet over medium heat. Add the coconut oil and swirl to coat the pan. When the oil has melted, and add the onion and sauté for 7 minutes, or until the onion is soft and translucent. Season with salt and pepper.

3. Add the ginger and garlic and sauté for 1 minute, until fragrant. Add the tomato paste and cook for 2 minutes, stirring the tomato paste into the onion. Add the coconut milk and curry powder and stir. Lower the heat to low, lightly season with salt and pepper, and simmer for 5 minutes.

4. While the curry is simmering, drain the rice and transfer to a saucepan. Add a pinch of salt and the water. Cover and bring to a boil over medium-high heat. As soon as the water boils, lower the heat to low and continue to simmer for 10 minutes.

5. While the rice is cooking, slip the catfish pieces into the curry and simmer for 10 to 12 minutes, until an instant-read thermometer inserted into the thickest part of the fish reads 145°F and the flesh is opaque and flakes with a fork.

6. To serve, spoon a portion of rice into shallow bowls and ladle the fish and curry over the rice. Garnish with the cilantro and serve immediately.

VARIATION 1 **CATFISH CURRY WITH GREEN BEANS AND SPINACH:** Bulk up the vegetables by adding 1 cup of trimmed green beans and chopped spinach to the curry. Add the vegetables at least 5 minutes before you add the fish to simmer.

VARIATION 2 **SHRIMP OR TILAPIA CURRY WITH BASMATI RICE:** This is an excellent dish to substitute shrimp or tilapia. Tilapia will cook within the same time as catfish; cook the shrimp in the curry until it is opaque and pink, 5 to 7 minutes depending on the size of the shrimp.

CATFISH FILLET WITH BABY KALE AND WILD RICE

A sheet pan supper is one in which almost all of the cooking is done from a single heat source and cookware. It's the quickest and most efficient way to have a healthy, filling, and quick dinner without much preparation. I love tossing raw baby kale into the roasted vegetables for color and more nutrient density. The residual heat from the roasted vegetables helps to soften and wilt the kale without having to cook it. **SERVES 4**

PREP TIME: 10 minutes
COOK TIME: 25 minutes

1 cup halved
grape tomatoes

1 medium zucchini, cut into
½-inch rounds

½ medium red onion, cut
into ¼-inch strips

4 tablespoons extra-virgin
olive oil, divided

Kosher salt

Freshly ground
black pepper

4 catfish fillets (1½ pound),
patted dry

Zest and juice of 1 lemon

1½ cups cooked wild rice

3 handfuls baby kale

1. Preheat the oven to 400°F. Line a baking sheet with parchment paper or aluminum foil.

2. Toss the tomatoes, zucchini, onion, and 2 tablespoons of olive oil together on the prepared baking sheet. Generously season with salt and pepper. Spread the vegetables in a single layer, leaving a space in the center for the fish, and roast for 10 minutes.

3. Drizzle 1 tablespoon of olive oil over the catfish and season both sides with salt and pepper.

4. Remove the baking sheet from the oven and place the fish in the center of the pan. Drizzle the lemon juice over the fish and return to the oven. Roast for 10 minutes, or until the fish is tender and flaky.

5. While the fish is roasting, in a large bowl, toss the lemon zest, wild rice, and kale together with the remaining 1 tablespoon of olive oil.

6. Transfer the roasted vegetables to the wild rice salad and toss gently to combine. Divide the salad among serving plates. Gently lift the catfish from the pan and place on top of each salad. Drizzle the juices from the baking sheet over the fish and serve immediately.

VARIATION 1 SALMON OR MACKEREL FILLET WITH WILD RICE: This sheet pan supper can be adapted for any type of fish—salmon and mackerel would be terrific with hearty chunks of red onion, grape tomatoes, and mushrooms.

VARIATION 2 ASIAN-STYLE CATFISH: Another great baking sheet recipe is roasted catfish with Asian vegetables. Toss shiitake mushrooms, carrots, red bell peppers, and bok choy with soy sauce and vegetable oil. Fold in some spinach and serve with steamed brown rice.

CHILI-LIME CATFISH WITH CHARRED CORN SALAD

Preparing dinner can be a sensory vacation. Break up the dinner bore-dom, leave behind your routine ingredients, and take up new ones for a nice change. Take this Mexican-inspired recipe for example: Lime juice punctuates this tasty fish recipe, while the charred corn and pasilla pepper's gentle heat work together with the chili powder on the mild catfish.

SERVES 4

PREP TIME: 10 minutes
COOK TIME: 20 minutes

¼ cup extra-virgin olive oil, divided

1 pasilla pepper, cut into ¼-inch dice

Kosher salt

Freshly ground black pepper

1 large shallot, thinly sliced

2 large garlic cloves, minced

2 cups frozen yellow corn kernels, thawed

Zest of 2 limes

Juice of 3 limes, divided

4 (6-ounce) catfish fillets

1 tablespoon chili powder

¼ cup coarsely chopped fresh cilantro leaves, divided

2 large handfuls baby arugula

1. Preheat the broiler. Line a baking sheet with aluminum foil.

2. To make the salad, in a cast iron skillet, heat 2 tablespoons of olive oil over medium-high heat. When shimmery wavy lines run through the oil, add the pasilla pepper and season with salt and pepper. Cook until the peppers become soft, about 4 minutes. Add the shallot and garlic and sauté for 1 minute, until the garlic is fragrant.

3. Add the corn and lightly season with salt and pepper. Continue to cook, stirring occasionally, until the corn begins to char slightly, 5 to 7 minutes. Some of the kernels may actually pop. Remove from the heat and stir in the lime zest and the juice of two limes.

4. To make the catfish, while the corn is charring, season the fillets on both sides with chili powder, salt, and pepper, then drizzle with the remaining 2 tablespoons of olive oil.

5. Place the fillets on the prepared baking sheet and broil for 6 to 7 minutes, or until an instant-read thermometer inserted into the thickest part of the fish reads 145°F. Remove from the oven and let the fish rest for 1 minute.

6. Toss 3 tablespoons of cilantro and the arugula with the corn salad, then divide evenly among plates. Place a piece of catfish on each salad. Squeeze the juice of the remaining lime over each plate and garnish with the remaining 1 tablespoon of cilantro. Serve immediately.

VARIATION 1 CHILI-LIME CATFISH TACOS: Break up the fillets and serve them with the salad folded into warm corn tortillas to morph this catfish dish into catfish tacos.

VARIATION 2 CHILI-LIME TILAPIA OR SHRIMP: Tilapia would work well in this recipe, as would shrimp. Tilapia's cooking time is similar to catfish; however, if you are using shrimp, cook for 4 to 6 minutes depending on their size.

CORNMEAL-FRIED CATFISH SANDWICHES

Also known as a Po' Boy, this crunchy fried catfish sandwiched in a crusty French roll with a lemony mayonnaise is a satisfying combination of flavors and textures. Adding cornstarch to the breading will result in a lighter, crispier exterior texture. **SERVES 4**

PREP TIME: 15 minutes
COOK TIME: 15 minutes

½ cup mayonnaise

Zest and juice of 1 lemon

2 teaspoons finely chopped capers

1 teaspoon Old Bay seasoning

½ teaspoon hot sauce (such as Tabasco or Crystal)

Kosher salt

Freshly ground black pepper

Vegetable oil, for frying

2 large eggs, beaten

1½ cups medium-ground cornmeal

½ cup all-purpose flour

¼ cup cornstarch

4 catfish fillets (1½ pound), trimmed to fit the length of the rolls

4 French bread sandwich rolls

4 green leaf lettuce leaves

2 Roma tomatoes, each cut into 6 slices

1. Preheat the oven to 350°F.

2. In a small mixing bowl, combine the mayonnaise, lemon zest, lemon juice, capers, Old Bay, and hot sauce. Season with salt and pepper. Cover with plastic wrap and refrigerate until ready to use.

3. In a cast iron skillet, heat ½ inch of vegetable oil over medium-high heat to 375°F, or when the end of a wooden spoon dipped into the oil causes bubbling and sizzling.

4. While the oil is heating, in a wide shallow bowl, beat the eggs. In another wide shallow bowl, combine the cornmeal, flour, and cornstarch.

5. When the oil is ready, season the catfish on both sides with salt and pepper. One at a time, dip the fillets into the egg, then coat in the cornmeal mixture and shake off the excess.

6. Lower the fish into the oil, letting it fall away from you. Fry the fillets for 3 to 4 minutes on each side, or until golden. Transfer the fillets to a plate lined with paper towels and season with kosher salt.

7. Split the rolls horizontally in half and toast lightly in the oven, about 7 to 8 minutes. Remove from the oven and spread the mayonnaise mixture on both sides, top with a fried catfish fillet, then top with the lettuce and tomato. Serve each sandwich sliced in half.

VARIATION 1 OPEN-FACED CATFISH SANDWICH: Serve these sandwiches open-faced on grilled sliced sourdough bread. Skip the lemon-caper mayonnaise and make a quick tartar sauce by mixing together 2 tablespoons of pickle relish into the mayonnaise.

VARIATION 2 CAJUN CORNMEAL-FRIED CATFISH SANDWICHES: Use tilapia, trout, or salmon. Spice it up by adding a Cajun spice mixture to the cornmeal dredging mixture.

PECAN-CRUSTED CATFISH

The pairing of catfish and pecans is an intersection of two very common and delicious elements in New Orleans food history. This recipe is a baked version, which is much lighter than the panfried versions. Serve it with some steamed rice and sautéed spinach for a well-rounded dinner.

SERVES 4

PREP TIME: 20 minutes
COOK TIME: 20 minutes

2 tablespoons unsalted butter, melted

¼ cup all-purpose flour

½ teaspoon ground nutmeg

Kosher salt

Freshly ground black pepper

2 large eggs, beaten

½ cup panko bread crumbs

½ cup finely chopped pecans

Zest and juice of 1 lemon, divided

4 (6-ounce) catfish fillets

1 lemon, quartered, for serving

1. Preheat the oven to 425°F. Line a baking sheet with aluminum foil and brush the bottom of the pan with the butter. Set aside.

2. In a wide shallow bowl, stir together the flour, nutmeg, and a pinch each of salt and pepper.

3. In another wide shallow bowl, beat the eggs. In a third wide shallow bowl or large plate, stir together the bread crumbs, pecans, and lemon zest.

4. Blot the fillets with paper towels and season both sides with salt and pepper. One at time, dredge the fillets in the flour mixture and shake off the excess.

5. Dip the fillets into the egg mixture and coat in the pecan mixture. Place the fillets on the prepared baking sheet.

6. Bake the fish for 15 minutes, rotating the pan halfway through, until an instant-read thermometer inserted into the thickest part of the fish reads 145°F and it flakes easily with a fork. Tent with foil to rest for 5 minutes.

7. Serve the fillets hot on plates garnished with the lemon wedges for squeezing.

VARIATION 1 ALMOND- OR HAZELNUT-CRUSTED WHITEFISH: Change up the nuts by using finely chopped almonds or hazelnuts instead. Tilapia and trout work well as substitutes for the catfish.

VARIATION 2 TROPICAL CATFISH: A tropical version can be made from a mixture of shredded coconut and chopped macadamia nuts instead of the bread crumbs and pecans. Lime juice enhances this variation better than lemon.

KUNG PAO CATFISH

This is a riff on kung pao chicken, which is best served with heaps of steamed rice. The benefit to making this at home is you can make it as mild or as hot as you like by adjusting the amount of chiles. The optional Szechuan peppercorns provide a mouth-numbing sensation, which can help create a buffer between your taste buds and the chiles. It's a multiple-step process because the catfish needs to be fried before being added to the sauce, but believe me, it's totally worth it. **SERVES 4**

PREP TIME: 15 minutes
COOK TIME: 20 minutes

FOR THE CATFISH

1½ pounds catfish fillets, cut into 1-inch chunks

2 tablespoons cornstarch

1 tablespoon egg white, lightly beaten until frothy

1 teaspoon soy sauce

2 cups vegetable oil

FOR THE KUNG PAO SAUCE

1 tablespoon Chinese black vinegar

1 teaspoon light soy sauce

1 teaspoon hoisin sauce

1 teaspoon sesame oil

1 teaspoon cornstarch

½ teaspoon ground Sichuan pepper (optional) ❯

1. To make the catfish, in a large bowl, toss the catfish with the cornstarch, egg white, and soy sauce. Make sure the fish is evenly coated with the mixture. Set aside for 10 minutes.

2. In a wok, large sauté pan, or skillet, heat the vegetable oil over medium-high heat to 325°F, or when the end of a wooden spoon dipped into the oil causes bubbling and sizzling.

3. Working in batches to avoid overcrowding, carefully lower the fish into the oil and gently move it around so it doesn't stick to the sides of the pan. Fry for about 2 minutes on each side, using a fish spatula or slotted spoon to flip the fish over, until golden. Transfer the fish to a plate lines with paper towels. Discard the oil and wipe out the wok.

4. To make the kung pao sauce, in a small bowl, combine the black vinegar, soy sauce, hoisin sauce, sesame oil, cornstarch, and Sichuan pepper (if using). Stir until the cornstarch is blended and set aside.

FOR THE STIR-FRY

2 tablespoons vegetable oil

8 to 10 dried red chiles

3 scallions, thinly sliced, divided (white and green parts)

2 garlic cloves, minced

1 teaspoon grated peeled fresh ginger

¼ cup unsalted dry-roasted peanuts

Steamed rice

5. To make the stir-fry, return the wok to medium-high heat until a bead of water sizzles and evaporates on contact. Add the vegetable oil and swirl to coat the bottom. Add the chiles and stir-fry for about 30 seconds, or until the chiles have just begun to blacken and the oil is slightly fragrant. (You may need to turn on your stove's exhaust fan, because stir-frying dried chiles on high heat can get a little smoky.)

6. Add the scallion whites, garlic, and ginger and stir-fry for about 30 seconds. Pour in the sauce and mix to coat the other ingredients. Add the fried fish and gently toss to coat but don't break up the fish too much. Stir in the peanuts and cook for another 1 to 2 minutes. Transfer to a serving plate, sprinkle the scallion greens on top, and serve with steamed rice.

VARIATION 1 KUNG PAO CATFISH WITH VEGETABLES: Bulk up the vegetables and add some diced onion and red bell pepper to the stir-fry.

VARIATION 2 BLACK BEAN CATFISH WITH GREEN BEANS: If spicy kung pao isn't your thing, you can still fry the catfish according to this recipe and stir-fry green beans or sliced asparagus with a generous spoonful of black bean sauce. Any jar of black bean sauce from an Asian market would be perfect.

FRIED CATFISH CAKES WITH REMOULADE SAUCE

If cocktail sauce and tartar sauce had a baby, they would name it remoulade. Remoulade sauce pairs beautifully with fried seafood, especially Cajun-inspired foods. If you have any leftover catfish from a previous recipe, use it to make these catfish cakes for an appetizer. Add a side salad or some vinegary coleslaw to round it out.

SERVES 4, AS AN APPETIZER

PREP TIME: 15 minutes
COOK TIME: 25 minutes

**FOR THE
REMOULADE SAUCE**

½ cup mayonnaise

1 scallion, finely chopped
(white and green parts)

1 tablespoon
prepared horseradish

2 teaspoons
whole-grain mustard

2 teaspoons hot sauce
(such as Tabasco)

2 teaspoons freshly
squeezed lemon juice

Kosher salt

Freshly ground
black pepper ❯

1. To make the remoulade sauce, in a small bowl, stir together the mayonnaise, scallion, horseradish, mustard, hot sauce, and lemon juice. Season with salt and pepper. Cover with plastic wrap and refrigerate until ready to use.

2. To make the catfish cakes, in a nonstick skillet, melt the butter over medium-low heat. Add the onion and garlic and cook until tender, about 4 minutes. Sprinkle in the flour and Old Bay and cook until a paste forms, about 2 minutes. Whisk in the milk until a thick sauce develops. Lightly season with salt and pepper and remove the pan from the heat.

3. Add the catfish to the pan and fold in gently. Add ¾ cup of bread crumbs and the parsley. Season with salt and pepper. Shape the mixture into 12 equal patties. Transfer the patties to a plate and refrigerate for 15 minutes.

4. In a large Dutch oven, heat the vegetable oil over medium heat to 350°F, or when the end of a wooden spoon dipped into the oil causes bubbling and sizzling.

FOR THE CATFISH CAKES

2 tablespoons
unsalted butter

½ small yellow
onion, grated

2 garlic cloves, minced

2 tablespoons
all-purpose flour

1 teaspoon Old
Bay seasoning

½ cup milk

Kosher salt

Freshly ground
black pepper

1 (8-ounce) catfish fillet,
cooked and flaked

2 cups panko bread
crumbs, divided

1 tablespoon minced fresh
flat-leaf parsley

2½ cups vegetable oil,
for frying

1 large egg, beaten

5. While the oil is heating, set up a dredging station. Beat the egg in a shallow bowl. In another shallow bowl, add the remaining 1¼ cups of bread crumbs. Working in batches, dip the patties in the egg, then dredge in the bread crumbs. Press the bread crumbs gently into the patties and place on another plate.

6. Working in batches, lower 3 or 4 cakes into the oil and cook for about 2 minutes. Flip the patties over and cook for another 2 minutes, until golden brown. Transfer the cakes to a plate lined with paper towels to drain. Season with salt and serve warm with the remoulade sauce.

VARIATION 1 FRIED CRAB CAKES WITH REMOULADE SAUCE: This fish cake recipe works great using flaked tilapia or crabmeat.

VARIATION 2 FRIED CATFISH CROQUETTES: Instead of forming into cakes, you can scoop out the mixture and form lime-size balls for catfish croquettes. Fry in oil until golden brown all the way around, about 3 minutes.

CARAMEL SIMMERED CATFISH (CA KHO TO)

This Vietnamese recipe is traditionally cooked in a clay pot, but I have a secret for you: In most restaurants, they only serve the dish in a clay pot at the table. Most of the time, it's cooked in conventional saucepans back in the kitchen. I find it even easier to cook in a nonstick pan! **SERVES 4**

PREP TIME: 10 minutes
COOK TIME: 35 minutes

2 catfish fillets (1½ pound), cut into 4 equal pieces

1 teaspoon Chinese five-spice powder

1 tablespoon fish sauce

Kosher salt

Freshly ground black pepper

2 tablespoons vegetable oil

1 small shallot, thinly sliced

4 garlic cloves, thinly sliced

1 red Fresno pepper, thinly sliced

1 cup coconut water

4 tablespoons sugar

2 tablespoons water

Juice of 1 lime, for garnish

1 tablespoon chopped fresh cilantro, for garnish

Steamed rice, for serving

1. Blot the catfish with paper towels and place in a bowl. Season with the five-spice powder, fish sauce, salt, and pepper. Marinate for 5 to 10 minutes.

2. In a nonstick skillet, heat the oil over medium-high heat. Add the shallot and garlic and sauté until they turn brown, about 1 minute. Add the Fresno pepper and sauté for 1 more minute.

3. Push the vegetables to the side of the pan and sear the catfish on both sides, about 3 minutes per side, until golden brown. Add the coconut water and lower the heat to medium-low. Braise the fish in the simmering coconut water while you prepare the sauce.

4. In a small saucepan or nonstick skillet, heat the sugar and water over medium-high heat until the mixture starts to bubble and begins to caramelize, about 6 to 7 minutes. Immediately pour it over the fish.

5. Simmer the fish in the caramel sauce for 20 minutes, or until the sauce thickens and the fish has taken on a deep caramelized color.

6. Transfer the fish and sauce to bowls. Garnish with the lime juice and cilantro. Serve with steamed rice.

VARIATION 1 CARAMEL SIMMERED TILAPIA: Tilapia is a good substitute for catfish in this recipe.

VARIATION 2 BACON AND CARAMEL SAUCE: Chop three thick-cut bacon slices and cook until chewy. Pour off the bacon fat and add the cooked bacon to the pan after the catfish has been seared. Simmer together in the coconut and caramel sauce.

Smoked Trout and Horseradish on Pumpernickel Toast, page 117

CHAPTER 7

TROUT

Trout is a freshwater fish native to North America and can be found in cold streams, rivers, and lakes. Varieties include rainbow, lake, brook, and several others. Those of us who can't fish for trout turn to the market, where fresh, frozen, and smoked trout are readily available. The most common variety available is rainbow trout. Trout's closest saltwater relative is salmon. In fact, steelhead trout move from freshwater to the ocean via the same rivers as the Pacific salmon.

Trout, like catfish, is a large commercial industry in North America dating back to the 1880s, when the first trout hatchery was founded. Nearly 70 percent of all rainbow trout raised in the US comes from farms in Idaho, where some of the trout are released into rivers and streams to compensate for overfishing.

The meat of the rainbow trout is delicate, tender, and flaky with a mild and subtle nutty flavor. Some rainbow trout flesh can have a pink or orange color due to the pigment in the food they are fed. When shopping, choose sustainably farmed trout from northern US states.

TROUT AMANDINE

The word "amandine" is French for "garnished with almonds." This dish is a variation of the French meunière dish, where the fish is dredged in flour, cooked, and served swimming in brown butter. Pairing almonds with the browned butter intensifies the butter's nuttiness and goes so well with the trout. It's a classic preparation. **SERVES 4**

PREP TIME: 15 minutes
COOK TIME: 20 minutes

4 tablespoons (½ stick) unsalted butter, divided

¼ cup sliced almonds

4 small rainbow trout (1½ pound), skin on, butterflied, and boned

Kosher salt

Freshly ground black pepper

½ cup all-purpose flour

½ cup almond flour

3 tablespoons vegetable oil

¼ cup finely chopped fresh flat-leaf parsley

Juice of 1 large lemon (about 2 to 3 tablespoons)

1. Preheat the oven to 300°F.

2. In a nonstick skillet, melt 2 tablespoons of butter over medium-high heat. Add the almonds and cook, stirring occasionally, until the almonds begin to look toasty brown. Transfer to a bowl and set aside.

3. Blot the fish with paper towels and season both sides with salt and pepper. In a wide shallow bowl, combine the all-purpose and almond flours, then dredge the fish on all sides, making sure it is completely coated.

4. In a skillet over medium-high heat, add the vegetable oil and swirl to coat the pan. When the oil reaches its smoke point, place the fish, flesh-side down, in the skillet and tilt the pan a few times to run the oil underneath the fish. Cook until the fish develops a golden crust, about 3 minutes. Carefully flip and cook for 1 minute on the skin side.

5. Transfer the fish to a plate and place in in the oven to keep warm. Pour the oil into a glass bowl and set aside to cool completely before discarding. Do not wipe out the pan, but let the pan cool for about 5 minutes before moving on.

6. Return the pan to medium heat and melt the remaining 2 tablespoons of butter. Continue to cook the butter until the milk solids begin to turn golden brown and smell nutty.

7. Remove from the heat and add the parsley. Let it sizzle before adding the lemon juice. Season the brown butter with salt and pepper and stir in the almonds.

8. Transfer the fish to serving plates and spoon the brown butter, parsley, and almonds over the fish. Serve hot.

VARIATION 1 **TROUT AMANDINE WITH TOMATO BUTTER:** Add a deliciously savory tomato butter to the trout amandine. Toss in a handful of grape tomatoes while the butter is melting. As the tomatoes cook, they will burst and break down, combining themselves with the butter and making a rustic sauce.

VARIATION 2 **HAZELNUT- OR PISTACHIO-TOPPED WHITEFISH:** Substitute hazelnuts or pistachios for the almonds and substitute the trout with tilapia, catfish, or mackerel. You can also add seasonings, such as a Cajun seasoning, to the dredging flour.

BACON-WRAPPED TROUT

This recipe is inspired by a scene in George R. R. Martin's *A Clash of Kings*, the second book from the series that informed the TV show *Game of Thrones*. There are riverlands in the realm of Westeros, so it stands to reason trout would appear on their dinner tables. Even if you aren't a fan or even a follower of this series, the simplicity of this recipe is unmistakable and lends truth to the saying "Bacon makes everything better."

SERVES 4

PREP TIME: 15 minutes
COOK TIME: 20 minutes

4 whole trout
(2 pounds), butterflied

2 tablespoons extra-virgin
olive oil

Kosher salt

Freshly ground
black pepper

4 thyme sprigs

4 dill sprigs

2 lemons, each thinly sliced
(total of 8 to 12 slices)

8 thick-cut bacon
slices (applewood
smoked preferred)

1. Preheat the oven to 425°F. Line a baking sheet with aluminum foil or parchment paper.

2. Blot the trout with paper towels. Drizzle the trout with the olive oil and season with salt and pepper on both sides.

3. Stuff each trout with a sprig of thyme, a sprig of dill, and two lemon slices. Fold the fish closed and wrap two bacon slices around each fish, tucking the ends underneath.

4. Place each trout, bacon ends down, on the prepared baking sheet and roast for 12 to 15 minutes. Adjust the oven to broil and continue to cook until the bacon is golden and crispy, 2 to 3 minutes. Watch carefully so that the bacon does not burn.

5. To serve, transfer each fish to warm serving plates and serve hot.

VARIATION 1 ITALIAN-STYLE TROUT: Make an Italian version using lemons, blood oranges, and rosemary, and wrap the fish with prosciutto instead of bacon.

VARIATION 2 BACON-WRAPPED SARDINES: Sardines wrapped in bacon are great. Use fresh butterflied sardines.

PAN-SEARED TROUT WITH GARLIC, BUTTER, AND THYME

Basic cooking lessons teach you how to pan sear a piece of chicken or steak and to make a simple sauce with the drippings and oil from the pan. Fish and seafood are no exception. The key is that the protein has to rest after being seared, and in the time it takes to rest, a delicious sauce can be made from what is left in the pan by adding just a few more ingredients. **SERVES 4**

PREP TIME: 10 minutes
COOK TIME: 20 minutes

4 (5-ounce) rainbow trout fillets

Kosher salt

Freshly ground black pepper

2 tablespoons extra-virgin olive oil

3 tablespoons unsalted butter, divided

4 large garlic cloves, thinly sliced

¼ cup dry white wine (such as Sauvignon blanc)

Zest and juice of 1 lemon

2 teaspoons chopped fresh thyme leaves

2 tablespoons coarsely chopped fresh flat-leaf parsley

1. Heat a 12-inch nonstick skillet over medium-high heat. While the pan is heating, generously season both sides of the fillets with salt and pepper.

2. When the pan is just barely smoking, heat the olive oil and 2 tablespoons of butter and swirl the pan to combine. Lower the heat to medium and place the fish, flesh-side down, in the pan. Cook for 4 to 5 minutes, or until the fish develops a golden crust. Carefully flip the fish over and sear the skin for another 2 minutes.

3. Transfer the fish to a plate and tent with aluminum foil.

4. In the same pan, still over medium heat, add the garlic and sauté for 1 minute, or until fragrant. Add the wine, lemon zest and juice, and thyme, stirring with a wooden spoon to scrape up any brown bits stuck to the pan. Simmer the wine mixture for about 2 minutes, until the liquid reduces by half. ❯

5. Remove from the heat and swirl in the remaining 1 tablespoon of butter until it melts and creates a velvety sauce. Return the fish to the pan and spoon the sauce over it.

6. To serve, drizzle the sauce over the top of the fillets. Garnish with the parsley and serve hot.

VARIATION 1 GREEK-STYLE PAN-SEARED TROUT: Add some sliced olives and fresh oregano to the sauce for a Greek twist.

VARIATION 2 ITALIAN-STYLE PAN-SEARED TROUT: Change up the flavors by using chopped rosemary instead of thyme and a handful of halved grape tomatoes and chopped capers.

SALT-BAKED TROUT WITH TARRAGON AND WINE

This dish is a dramatic way to cook and present a whole fish. Baking fish encased in a salt crust is an ancient cooking method. The earliest documented version of this method is from the fourth century BCE and details a whole fish stuffed with herbs and lemon then packed in a crust made from salt and egg whites. This technique is used commonly around the world because it does three very important things all at once: It roasts, steams, and seasons the food in a very short period of time. **SERVES 4**

PREP TIME: 20 minutes
COOK TIME: 40 minutes

2 whole trout (2 pounds), butterflied and boned

2 tablespoons dry white wine (such as Sauvignon blanc)

Freshly ground black pepper

6 tarragon sprigs, plus more for garnish

1 lemon, thinly sliced

6 cups kosher salt

4 large egg whites, beaten until frothy

1. Preheat the oven to 475°F. Line a baking sheet with parchment paper or aluminum foil.

2. Open the trout, drizzle with the wine, and lightly season with pepper. Stuff each fish with the tarragon and lemon slices and fold them closed. Secure each trout closed with toothpicks.

3. In a bowl, mix the salt and egg whites together until it resembles the texture of wet sand. On the baking sheet, spread 2 cups of the salt mixture in a thick even layer. Place the fish on the salt bed, side by side, with a 2-inch space between them.

4. Cover each trout with 1 cup of the salt mixture, packing the salt to cover the fish entirely. Use the remaining salt to cover in any gaps.

5. Bake the fish for 25 to 30 minutes, or until the salt begins to turn golden brown. Remove the pan from the oven and let it cool for 10 minutes. ❯

6. Carefully break the salt crust around the top half of each fish and lift the "lid" off the fish. Lift each trout from the salt bed and transfer to a plate, removing the toothpicks and scraping away the tarragon and lemon. Garnish with more pepper and tarragon. Serve hot.

VARIATION 1 SALT-BAKED TROUT WITH LEMON, THYME, AND PARSLEY: Stuff the fish with lemon and herbs such as thyme, parsley, or dill instead of the tarragon and wine.

VARIATION 2 TROUT SALAD: Leftover fish can be turned into a fantastic salad with chopped celery, parsley, 1 teaspoon of mustard, and a couple tablespoons of mayonnaise.

CAMPFIRE TROUT IN FOIL PACKETS

If you go camping, then I'm sure you are familiar with cooking food in foil packets over a campfire. What I love about this technique is that it's a derivative of fish en papillote, using foil instead of parchment paper. You can cook an entire meal—with starches, vegetables, and protein all together—with just one pouch and a single heat source. **SERVES 4**

PREP TIME: 15 minutes
COOK TIME: 20 minutes

4 whole trout
(2 pounds), butterflied

Kosher salt

Freshly ground
black pepper

Nonstick cooking spray

2 carrots, peeled and cut
into ¼-inch-thick coins

1 leek, trimmed and
thinly sliced

1 lemon, cut into ¼-inch-
thick slices (about 6 slices)

4 dill or thyme sprigs

4 tablespoons (½ stick)
unsalted butter

1. Preheat the broiler.

2. Season the fish on both sides with salt and pepper.

3. Place two sheets of aluminum foil on top of each other and lightly spray the center with nonstick cooking spray. Make a bed from one-quarter of the carrots and leeks and lightly season with salt and pepper. Place one fish, opened and skin-side down, on the vegetables.

4. Top with a slice of lemon and a sprig of dill. Place 1 tablespoon of butter on the fish and close the fish. Fold and seal the foil into an airtight package. Repeat the process with the remaining fish, carrots, leek, lemon, dill, and butter.

5. Place the fish packets on a baking sheet and cook, turning once, for 15 to 20 minutes, or until the skin peels away from the fish and the flesh is flaky.

6. Open the packets carefully, as the steam can burn you, and place the entire foil packet on a plate. Serve hot.

VARIATION 1 SPANISH-STYLE CAMPFIRE TROUT: Make Spanish-style foil packets by sprinkling paprika and garlic over the fish and cooking with olives and tomatoes.

VARIATION 2 WASABI AND SOY TROUT PACKETS: Make a Japanese-inspired foil packet by stirring ½ teaspoon of wasabi into 3 teaspoons of soy sauce. Drizzle the mixture over the fish and cook with ginger and sesame seeds.

CEDAR PLANK–GRILLED TROUT

Grilling on a cedar plank gives the trout a light smokiness, leaving the meat tender and moist. Keep a spray bottle filled with water nearby in case the plank begins to scorch. I specifically chose to keep the trout simple, so the cedar flavor comes through. If you don't have an outside grill, simply cook in a 450°F oven for 10 to 12 minutes. You'll still get that lovely cedar aroma. **SERVES 4**

PREP TIME: 2 hours
COOK TIME: 20 minutes

2 (10- to 12-ounce) whole trout, butterflied

Salt

Freshly ground black pepper

¼ cup extra-virgin olive oil

2 lemon, each cut into 6 slices

4 dill sprigs

1. Soak two (7-by-15-inch) cedar planks in cold water for up to 2 hours. Place a heavy pan on top of the planks to keep them submerged.

2. Heat an outdoor gas grill to medium-high or prepare coals to white ash for a charcoal grill.

3. Season both sides of the fish with salt and pepper and rub each with the olive oil. Set aside.

4. Place the soaked cedar planks on the grill over direct medium heat. When the cedar plank starts to smoke, place the fish on the planks and top with the lemons and dill.

5. Move the plank to indirect heat. Grill the fish for about 15 minutes, or until the flesh is opaque and flakes with a fork.

6. Transfer the fish from the planks to plates and serve hot.

VARIATION 1 DRY-RUBBED CEDAR PLANK–ROASTED TROUT: Use a dry rub on the fish before placing it on the plank for more flavor. Mix together ½ teaspoon each of paprika, cayenne pepper, ground cumin, and brown sugar.

VARIATION 2 MAPLE-GLAZED ROASTED TROUT: Omit the dill when cooking the trout on the cedar plank and prepare a glaze of maple syrup, vegetable oil, and 1 teaspoon of Dijon mustard.

SMOKED TROUT AND HORSERADISH ON PUMPERNICKEL TOAST

Open-faced sandwiches, or smørrebrød, appear again here in the trout chapter because smoked trout is incredibly delicious with pumpernickel bread. Smørrebrød (see page 51) is a terrific way to use up leftover bits and pieces on top of buttered bread. Experiment with different toppings to create your own delicious combinations. **SERVES 4**

PREP TIME: 15 minutes
COOK TIME: 5 minutes

2 slices whole-grain pumpernickel rye bread, halved

2 tablespoons unsalted butter, at room temperature

½ cup mayonnaise

1 tablespoon prepared horseradish

1 tablespoon finely chopped fresh dill

Zest of 1 lemon

Kosher salt

Freshly ground black pepper

6 ounces smoked trout, flaked

4 grape tomatoes, thinly sliced, for garnish

1 tablespoon thinly sliced fresh chives, for garnish

1. Toast the pumpernickel lightly and set aside to cool. On each toast, spread a thin layer of the butter and place on a platter or cutting board.

2. In a small bowl, stir together the mayonnaise, horseradish, dill, lemon zest, and a pinch each of salt and pepper. Spread the mayonnaise mixture over each toast.

3. Top each toast with the smoked trout and garnish with the tomato and chives. Serve immediately.

VARIATION 1 SMOKED SALMON OR TUNA ON BRIOCHE: Smoked salmon or oil-poached tuna would be terrific substitutes for trout. Slices of buttery brioche sandwich bread would make a great base if you can't find the pumpernickel bread.

VARIATION 2 SMOKED TROUT AND APPLE SANDWICH: Try adding a fruit to the sandwich by placing some sliced green apple on the bread. The combination of savory and sweet is beautifully satisfying.

ROASTED TROUT AND BLACK LENTIL SALAD

Nutty and chewy, lentils pair wonderfully with delicate flaky trout. Beluga lentils are tiny, round, and black. They get their name because they resemble beluga caviar. They are delicious, but I'll admit they are hard to find. Any lentil will do but keep in mind the brown lentils can break down to mush if overcooked. **SERVES 4**

PREP TIME: 10 minutes
COOK TIME: 45 minutes

FOR THE DRESSING

1 tablespoon white wine vinegar

1 tablespoon extra-virgin olive oil

1 teaspoon Dijon mustard

1 teaspoon honey

Kosher salt

Freshly ground black pepper

FOR THE LENTILS AND TROUT

1½ cups dried beluga lentils, picked through and rinsed

4 (6- to 7-ounce) trout fillets

2 tablespoons extra-virgin olive oil

Kosher salt

Freshly ground black pepper

6 ounces baby spinach

1 to 2 teaspoons finely chopped fresh dill, for garnish

1. To make the dressing, in a small bowl, whisk together the vinegar, olive oil, mustard, and honey. Season with salt and pepper. Cover and refrigerate until ready to use.

2. To make the lentils, place them in a saucepan and cover with cold water. Bring to a boil over high heat, skimming off any foam that forms. Lower the heat to medium-low and simmer, stirring occasionally, for 20 to 25 minutes, until the lentils are tender but hold their shape. Add more water, if needed.

3. While the lentils cook, preheat the broiler. Line a baking sheet with aluminum foil.

4. To make the trout, place it skin-side down on the prepared baking sheet. Rub both sides with the olive oil and season with salt and pepper. Roast for 10 minutes, until an instant-read thermometer inserted into the thickest part of the fish reads 145°F and the flesh flakes easily with a fork. Remove from the oven and tent with foil.

5. When the lentils are cooked, drain any excess cooking water and transfer to a mixing bowl. Season with salt and pepper and drizzle in half the dressing and the spinach. The heat from the lentils will slightly wilt the spinach.

6. Divide the lentil salad among serving plates. Remove the skin from the trout. Place a fillet on top of each salad. Drizzle the tops of the fish with remaining dressing, garnish with the dill, and serve either hot or warm.

VARIATION 1 ASIAN-STYLE ROASTED TROUT AND BLACK LENTIL SALAD: Use wasabi in place of the mustard, along with 2 teaspoons of soy sauce, 1 tablespoon of rice vinegar, 1 teaspoon of sesame oil, and chopped cilantro to make a dressing.

VARIATION 2 ROASTED TROUT WITH BLACK LENTIL AND FARRO SALAD: Bulk up the entire dish and make it a truly hearty meal by tossing in 1 cup of cooked farro and add chopped tomatoes to the salad for more color and brightness.

Shrimp and Pineapple in Thai Red Curry, page 126

CHAPTER 8

SHRIMP

Nearly one-fourth of all seafood consumed in the United States is shrimp. Shrimp's deliciously mild and sweet flavor blends well with other flavors, and it's also an excellent source of protein and can help raise your good cholesterol levels (HDLs), which contributes to heart health.

Shrimp is available in medium, large, jumbo, and colossal sizes and is labeled as such, as well as how many shrimp of each size is in a pound. For example, "large" shrimp means a pound of this size should yield under 31 to 35 pieces. Recipes in this chapter will specify which sizes are best for texture, taste, and serving quantities.

Finding shrimp at the market is easy, but you need to know exactly what you need because they come in all forms: precooked, raw, fresh, frozen, and canned. For raw shrimp, you'll have the option of getting them shell on, peeled, tails on, tails off, and deveined. Choose shrimp that has been farmed using recirculating tanks in the US or wild-caught shrimp from the waters in North America around the Southern Atlantic, the Gulf of Mexico, and the Pacific Ocean in the Baja region.

THE EASIEST SHRIMP COCKTAIL

This a contemporary take on a classic dish. Here, we roast the shrimp in the oven at a high temperature to avoid eating soggy, tasteless, overcooked, and watery shrimp. The cocktail sauce gets an update, too, using sriracha to give it a new spicy zip! **SERVES 4**

PREP TIME: 15 minutes
COOK TIME: 10 minutes

FOR THE COCKTAIL SAUCE

⅓ cup sriracha

½ cup ketchup

2 tablespoons prepared horseradish

Juice of ½ lemon

½ teaspoon Worcestershire sauce

FOR THE SHRIMP

2 pounds extra jumbo shrimp (U16/20), peeled, tails on, and deveined

1½ tablespoons extra-virgin olive oil

2 teaspoons kosher salt

½ teaspoon freshly ground black pepper

1. To make the cocktail sauce, in a small bowl, stir together the sriracha, ketchup, horseradish, lemon juice, and Worcestershire sauce. Cover with plastic wrap and refrigerate until ready to use.

2. Preheat the oven to 400°F. Line a baking sheet with aluminum foil or parchment paper.

3. To make the shrimp, in a small bowl, toss the shrimp with the olive oil, salt, and pepper. Let the shrimp marinate for 5 minutes. Spread the shrimp in a single layer on the prepared baking sheet.

4. Roast for 10 minutes, until the shrimp have turned just pink and opaque white. Remove from the oven and set aside to cool.

5. Smear a spoonful of sauce onto four chilled plates. Evenly divide the shrimp among the plates and serve immediately.

VARIATION 1 CAJUN SHRIMP COCKTAIL: Season the shrimp further by adding 2 teaspoons of Cajun seasoning or Old Bay when marinating.

VARIATION 2 LETTUCE-WRAPPED SHRIMP TACOS: Shrimp cocktail doesn't have to be simply a dip-and-eat experience. You can pile up the shrimp in lettuce cups and eat them like tacos.

SHRIMP RUMAKI (BACON-WRAPPED SHRIMP)

As the holidays approach, keep this recipe up your sleeve for when you need to pull out something special and unique. This recipe is a throwback to the 1950s and 1960s, when everything Polynesian was trendy. Rumaki is a classic dish normally made with water chestnuts and chicken livers wrapped in bacon. I decided to use shrimp instead of the chicken livers. You're welcome. **SERVES 6 TO 8, AS AN APPETIZER**

PREP TIME: 1 hour 15 minutes
COOK TIME: 25 minutes

½ cup seasoned rice vinegar

½ cup soy sauce

2 tablespoons sugar

2 teaspoons minced peeled fresh ginger

1 teaspoon sriracha

1 pound extra large shrimp (U26/30), shelled and deveined

2 (8-ounce) cans sliced water chestnuts, drained

4 scallions, cut into 4 (1-inch) pieces (white and green parts)

8 ounces bacon, each slice halved

1. In a bowl, stir together the rice vinegar, soy sauce, sugar, ginger, and sriracha until combined. Add the shrimp and toss to coat. Cover with plastic wrap and refrigerate for up to 1 hour. In another small bowl, cover 30 toothpicks with water and soak for 1 hour.

2. Preheat the oven to 450°F. Line a baking sheet with parchment paper or aluminum foil and set aside.

3. Drain the shrimp and discard the marinade. Place one shrimp and one piece of scallion in between two slices of water chestnuts. Wrap half of a bacon slice tightly around the shrimp and secure with a toothpick.

4. Place on the prepared baking sheet and repeat the process with the remaining shrimp, scallions, water chestnuts, and bacon. ❯

5. Roast the shrimp for 14 minutes, flipping them over once halfway through, or until the shrimp are opaque and the bacon is cooked thoroughly.

6. Adjust the oven to broil and broil the rumaki on high for 1 minute each side, flipping once, or until the bacon is crispy on both sides. Serve hot.

VARIATION 1 SCALLOP RUMAKI: Though this appetizer is about as decadent as it gets, replace the shrimp with scallops for next-level deliciousness and flavor.

VARIATION 2 SIMPLE BACON-WRAPPED SHRIMP: Simplify by wrapping the bacon around the shrimp and broiling. Fans of the character Ron Swanson from the TV show *Parks and Recreation* will approve!

GARLIC SHRIMP IN SHERRY SAUCE

The Spanish call this dish "gambas al ajillo." It's a simple dish that can be found in any tapas bar in Spain. Tapas (or "covers") were originally just slices of bread offered to travelers who stopped at bars for wine to place over their drinks to keep flies from falling in. Over the years, establishments began to add tasty spreads, and they eventually evolved into the small dishes with assertively flavored food on them that we now call tapas. **SERVES 4 TO 6, AS AN APPETIZER**

PREP TIME: 20 minutes
COOK TIME: 15 minutes

1 pound medium shrimp (U36/40), peeled, tail on, and deveined

Kosher salt

⅓ cup extra-virgin olive oil

6 large garlic cloves, thinly sliced

¼ cup minced fresh flat-leaf parsley

2 tablespoons dry sherry

1 teaspoon paprika or Spanish pimentón

¼ teaspoon cayenne pepper

1 baguette, cut into 16 thin slices and lightly toasted, for serving

1. Blot the shrimp on a bed of paper towels. Toss the shrimp with a ½ teaspoon of kosher salt.

2. In a large nonstick skillet over medium-high heat, combine the olive oil, garlic, and parsley. Cook until the garlic begins to sizzle, but be careful to avoid burning it. Immediately add the shrimp and cook for 2 to 3 minutes. Add the sherry, paprika, and cayenne, cooking until the shrimp is opaque and the sauce reduces slightly, about 1 minute more.

3. Transfer the shrimp and sauce to a serving dish. Serve with toasted baguette on the side.

VARIATION 1 **GARLIC SHRIMP IN A TOMATO SHERRY SAUCE:** Toss in 1 cup of halved grape tomatoes to sauté with the shrimp. The tomatoes will cook down and contribute to the sauce.

VARIATION 2 **GARLIC SHRIMP WITH ALMONDS:** Make the dish even richer by adding ¼ cup of sliced almonds when frying the garlic.

SHRIMP AND PINEAPPLE IN THAI RED CURRY

If you are craving something rich and satisfying with a deep balance of sweet, savory, and spicy, this recipe nails it. Plus, it's an easy introduction to cooking Thai food at home and takes very little time to complete. Get the rice cooking on the stove, and it will be ready when the curry is ready. Perfectly timed. **SERVES 4**

PREP TIME: 10 minutes
COOK TIME: 20 minutes

2 cups jasmine rice, rinsed

2 tablespoons coconut oil

2 tablespoons Thai red curry paste

1 cup coconut milk

1 pound medium shrimp (U36/40), peeled and deveined

1 cup pineapple chunks

1 tablespoon packed brown sugar

Zest and juice of 1 lime

2 teaspoons fish sauce

¼ cup roughly torn Thai basil leaves, for garnish

1. In a Dutch oven, cover the rice with cold water by 1 inch. Cover and bring to a boil over high heat. Immediately lower the heat to low and simmer for 12 to 15 minutes, until tender. When done, keep covered until ready to serve.

2. While the rice cooks, melt the coconut oil in large skillet over medium-high heat. Add the curry paste and sauté until fragrant, about 1 minute. Add the coconut milk and the shrimp and simmer for 5 minutes, or until the shrimp are pink. Stir in the pineapple and remove the pan from the heat. Stir in the brown sugar, lime zest and juice, and fish sauce.

3. To serve, divide the rice among warm bowls and spoon the curry over. Garnish with Thai basil and serve hot.

VARIATION 1 CATFISH AND PINEAPPLE THAI RED CURRY: You can substitute catfish for the shrimp. Cut the catfish fillets into bite-size chunks and simmer in the curry as you would the shrimp.

VARIATION 2 RED CURRY CLAMS: You can prepare the curry sauce (without the pineapple) in a Dutch oven or large sauté pan or skillet with a lid. Add 2 pounds of clams or mussels. Simmer on medium-high for 8 to 10 minutes for clams, 5 to 6 minutes for mussels.

BROILED SHRIMP SCAMPI

Scampi is actually another name for langoustine, a relative of our favorite shellfish, the shrimp. Here, it's referred to as the way the dish is prepared—with lots of garlic and butter. My preferred way to eat shrimp scampi is with lots of crusty bread so I can soak up the garlicky sauce, but I've also seen it on restaurant menus served over pasta. **SERVES 4**

PREP TIME: 10 minutes
COOK TIME: 10 minutes

1 tablespoon extra-virgin olive oil

4 tablespoons (½ stick) unsalted butter, at room temperature

⅓ cup chopped fresh flat-leaf parsley, divided

5 garlic cloves, minced

Red pepper flakes

Zest and juice of 1 lemon, divided

Kosher salt

Freshly ground black pepper

1½ pounds colossal shrimp (U13/15), shelled, tails on, deveined, and butterflied

Crusty bread, for serving

1. Preheat the broiler. Line a baking sheet with aluminum foil and rub with the olive oil.

2. In a small bowl, mix together the butter, half the parsley, the garlic, red pepper flakes, and lemon zest. Season with salt and pepper.

3. Arrange the shrimp, flattened out and tails up, in a single layer on the baking sheet. Season with salt and pepper and place a small dollop of the seasoned butter mixture in the center of each shrimp.

4. Broil for 5 to 6 minutes, or until the shrimp are opaque and sizzling. Transfer the shrimp to a platter. Garnish with the lemon juice and the remaining half of parsley. Serve immediately with crusty bread.

VARIATION 1 **SHRIMP SCAMPI LINGUINE:** If you sauté all of the ingredients with a ¼ cup of Pinot grigio in a sauté pan or skillet instead of the broiler, you have the makings of an excellent topping for a pasta dish. Linguine would be a fantastic pasta choice.

VARIATION 2 **BROILED CLAM OR MUSSEL SCAMPI:** These ingredients would also be amazing tossed with clams or mussels.

COCONUT SHRIMP WITH PINEAPPLE DIPPING SAUCE

Coconut shrimp is decadent but so easy to prepare and worth the extra step to butterfly them. Take a trip to the tropics in less than 30 minutes using only your taste buds. Here, I am offering an unusual dipping sauce that's sweet, hot, and tangy—all at the same time. **SERVES 4**

PREP TIME: 15 minutes
COOK TIME: 15 minutes

FOR THE DIPPING SAUCE

1 (8-ounce) can crushed pineapple, with its juices

1 tablespoon orange marmalade

Juice of ½ lime

1 teaspoon sriracha

FOR THE SHRIMP

½ cup cornstarch

½ teaspoon cayenne pepper

Kosher salt

2 cups unsweetened shredded coconut

3 large egg whites

24 uncooked jumbo shrimp (U16/20; about 1½ pounds), peeled, tails on, deveined, and butterflied

4 cups of vegetable oil, for deep frying

1. To make the dipping sauce, in a blender or food processor, blend the pineapple, marmalade, lime juice, and sriracha until smooth. Transfer to a bowl and cover with plastic wrap. Refrigerate until ready to use.

2. To make the shrimp, in a medium bowl, mix together the cornstarch and cayenne pepper. Season with salt. Place the coconut in a wide shallow dish. In another medium bowl, beat the egg whites until frothy and foamy.

3. One at a time, dredge the shrimp in the cornstarch mixture and shake off the excess. Dip the shrimp into the egg whites, then press the shrimp into the coconut, coating both sides. Transfer to a plate. Repeat the process with the remaining shrimp.

4. In a wide shallow stockpot over medium-high heat, heat the vegetable oil to 350°F, or when the end of a wooden spoon dipped into the oil causes bubbling and sizzling.

5. Working in batches, fry 4 to 5 shrimp until cooked through, about 1 to 2 minutes. You may need to flip them halfway through.

6. Transfer the shrimp to a plate lined with paper towels to drain. Lightly season with salt while still hot.

7. To serve, arrange the shrimp on a platter and serve with the dipping sauce on the side.

VARIATION 1 SWEETENED COCONUT SHRIMP: Make the coconut shrimp a touch sweeter by soaking the shrimp in 4 cups of cold water mixed with ¼ cup of sugar and 2 tablespoons of salt for 30 minutes. Brining the shrimp will introduce the sugar and salt deeper into the meat, making it more succulent and flavorful. You can also use half sweetened coconut and half unsweetened.

VARIATION 2 BAKED COCONUT SHRIMP: For a lighter version, spray an aluminum foil-lined baking sheet with nonstick cooking spray and arrange the breaded shrimp in a single layer. Bake for 8 to 12 minutes in a 400°F oven.

SHRIMP AND CHEESY GRITS

I often get asked to explain the difference between grits and polenta. They're both corn-based porridges, but grits are made from ground-up dried hominy, which is maize kernels that have been soaked in a lye solution. Polenta, on the other hand, is cornmeal. Either way, the corn flavor brings out the sweetness of the shrimp and adding bacon makes it rich and delicious. **SERVES 4 TO 6**

PREP TIME: 15 minutes
COOK TIME: 25 minutes

FOR THE GRITS

2 cups low-sodium chicken stock

2 cups whole milk

¾ cup old-fashioned grits

Kosher salt

Freshly ground black pepper

1 cup shredded Cheddar cheese

4 tablespoons (½ stick) unsalted butter, at room temperature and cubed

2 dashes hot sauce (such as Tabasco) ❯

1. To make the grits, in a 3-quart Dutch oven over medium-high heat, bring the stock and milk to a boil. Lower the heat to medium and stir in the grits in a steady stream. Continue to stir and cook until they begin to thicken. Season with salt and pepper.

2. Cover and lower the heat to low. Continue to cook, stirring occasionally, for 15 minutes, or until the liquid is completely absorbed.

3. Stir in the cheese, butter, and hot sauce. Remove from the heat, cover, and set aside while you make the shrimp.

4. To make the shrimp, in a large nonstick skillet over medium-high heat, cook the bacon until brown and crispy, about 7 minutes. Transfer the bacon to a plate lined with paper towels. Drain the bacon fat to a bowl.

5. In the same skillet heat 2 tablespoons of the bacon fat. Add the shrimp to the pan. Add the garlic and Cajun seasoning and sauté for 4 minutes, until the shrimp turn pink. Season with salt and pepper.

FOR THE SHRIMP

6 thick-cut bacon slices, cut into ½-inch-thick strips

1 pound medium shrimp (U36/40), peeled and deveined, and blotted dry.

4 large garlic cloves, thinly sliced

1 teaspoon Cajun seasoning

Kosher salt

Freshly ground black pepper

4 scallions, thinly sliced (white and green parts), for garnish

6. Remove from the heat, return the bacon to the pan, and toss together with the shrimp.

7. To serve, spoon the grits into serving bowls and top with shrimp and bacon. Garnish with the scallions and serve immediately.

VARIATION 1 ITALIAN-STYLE SHRIMP AND GRITS: You can make this with a twist of Italian flavors by using Parmesan cheese instead of Cheddar and pancetta instead of bacon. Top with a dollop of pesto sauce right on the sautéed shrimp.

VARIATION 2 SHRIMP AND GRITS WITH EGGS: If you're making shrimp and grits for breakfast, crown the dish with a fried or poached egg. The runny yolk makes the grits even more creamy-dreamy.

SHRIMP TEMPURA

Lightly battered, crispy fried shrimp—there's nothing like it. They key to this is understanding the science of batters and deep frying. Make sure the shrimp has been chilled and that the batter is mixed briefly with ice cold soda water before you begin to cook. Save this recipe for when you can leisurely cook this at home. This takes a bit of time and will make a slight mess of your kitchen, but it's worth the effort. **SERVES 4**

PREP TIME: 15 minutes
COOK TIME: 15 minutes

FOR THE DIPPING SAUCE

1 cup dashi soup stock

¼ cup seasoned
rice vinegar

¼ cup soy sauce

1½ teaspoons sugar

FOR THE SHRIMP

4 cups vegetable oil,
for frying

¾ cup rice flour

¼ cup cornstarch

⅛ teaspoon baking soda

Kosher salt

Pinch freshly ground
black pepper

1 pound extra jumbo
shrimp (U16/20), peeled,
deveined, and butterflied

1 large egg yolk

1 cup sparkling water,
ice cold

1. To make the dipping sauce, in a saucepan over medium-high heat, mix together the dashi, rice vinegar, soy sauce, and sugar and bring to a boil. Stir gently until the sugar dissolved. Transfer to a bowl and keep warm.

2. Set a wire rack over a baking sheet and set aside.

3. To make the shrimp, in a Dutch oven or wok over medium heat, heat the oil to 375°F, or when the end of a wooden spoon dipped into the oil causes bubbling and sizzling. While the oil is heating, in a medium bowl, whisk together the rice flour, cornstarch, baking soda, salt, and pepper. Set aside.

4. Blot the shrimp with paper towels and place on a plate. Lightly season both sides with salt and pepper. Transfer to the refrigerator.

5. Mix the egg yolk and sparkling water together, then pour the flour mixture in and whisk until just combined. Working in batches, dip each shrimp into the batter, shaking off the excess. Lower into the oil, making sure it drops away from you to avoid getting splashed.

6. Fry, 4 or 5 at a time so as not to cool down the oil too much, for 3 to 4 minutes, until the shrimp are golden brown and the batter has turned into a light, lacy, and crispy coating.

7. Using a wire skimmer, transfer the shrimp to the wire rack to drain. Lightly season with salt while still hot.

8. To serve, arrange the shrimp tempura on a warm platter with the dipping sauce on the side.

VARIATION 1 MACKEREL OR SALMON TEMPURA: You can tempura strips of salmon or mackerel, as well as vegetables like sliced carrot, sweet potato, asparagus, and green beans.

VARIATION 2 SPICY SHRIMP TEMPURA TACOS: Toss some thinly sliced red and green jalapeño peppers in the tempura batter and deep-fry along with the shrimp. Serve the shrimp and sliced jalapeños in warm corn tortillas.

Cioppino, page 145

CHAPTER 9

CRAB

There are over 4,000 different varieties of crab enjoyed around the world, but the most common ones we can get commercially are blue, Dungeness, snow, king, and spider. For recipes requiring full-size crab or crab pieces in their shells, look for whole fresh crab from the market, preferably during crab season. Crab season is in place to ensure that there are sustainable levels of crab, and it prevents crab species from becoming overfished.

Crab has as much protein as meat, but none of the saturated fats. Rich in vitamins and minerals, crab also has high levels of omega-3s, the kind that play a huge role in our heart health.

Crab season begins in late October and ends in early February. Season opening is determined by the size and population of adult crab available. When cooking with crab during the off-season, opt for canned crab or frozen crab. Make sustainable choices by choosing crab caught from Alaska, the US West Coast, and Maryland's Chesapeake Bay.

CRAB CAKES

Crab cakes originate from the mid-Atlantic seaboard, where blue crab is plentiful. These crabs are small, so it takes some effort to pick the meat from them. I recommend saving some energy by using the best quality canned crabmeat, which also saves time and money. Remember to chill the cakes in the refrigerator before you cook them so that the ingredients can retain their shape when you place them in the hot pan. **SERVES 4**

PREP TIME: 10 minutes, plus 1 hour to chill
COOK TIME: 10 minutes

½ cup mayonnaise

1 large egg, beaten

2 teaspoons Dijon mustard

1 teaspoon Worcestershire sauce

1 teaspoon Old Bay seasoning

1 (16-ounce) container lump crabmeat

12 saltine crackers, finely crushed

2 tablespoons chopped fresh flat-leaf parsley

Kosher salt

Freshly ground black pepper

2 tablespoons vegetable oil, for pan frying

1 lemon, quartered, for serving

1. In a medium bowl, whisk together the mayonnaise, egg, mustard, Worcestershire sauce, and Old Bay seasoning.

2. Add the crabmeat, cracker crumbs, and parsley. Fold gently to mix. Lightly season with salt and pepper. Divide into four equal portions and shape into cakes. Place the cakes on a plate and cover with plastic wrap. Refrigerate for at least 1 hour.

3. In a nonstick skillet over medium-high heat, heat the vegetable oil. When shimmery wavy lines run through the oil, place the cakes in the pan and fry for 6 to 7 minutes, flipping once halfway through, until each side is golden brown.

4. Transfer the crab cakes to warm plates and lightly season with salt while they are still hot. Serve hot with the lemon wedges for squeezing.

VARIATION 1 **CRAB CAKE EGGS BENEDICT:** Elevate your eggs Benedict game by serving crab cakes on them instead of Canadian bacon. The runny yolk and hollandaise sauce pairs beautifully with the sweet crab.

VARIATION 2 **FISH CAKES:** You can make fish cakes using this recipe with just about any cooked flaky fish, such as salmon, tuna, and catfish.

STEAMED DUNGENESS CRAB WITH OLD BAY BUTTER

If whole crab is being brought home to my family, this is how it will be prepared: steamed, then cracked and dipped in a flavorful butter. It's a delicious way to sit around the table and catch up on the week's events. Pull up a chair, spread out the mallets and nutcrackers, and tuck kitchen towels over your shirts. **SERVES 4**

PREP TIME: 10 minutes
COOK TIME: 20 minutes

2 bay leaves

Juice of 1 lemon

2 whole Dungeness crabs, (3–4 pounds) scrubbed clean

4 tablespoons (½ stick) unsalted butter, melted

1 tablespoon Old Bay seasoning

1. Pour two inches of water into a wide stock pot. Add the bay leaves and lemon juice. Set an expandable steaming basket in the pot and place the crabs in the basket. Bring the pot to a boil over high heat. Lower the heat to medium, cover, and steam for 15 to 20 minutes, until the crabs are bright orange.

2. While the crabs are steaming, in a small bowl, stir together the butter and Old Bay seasoning and set aside.

3. Transfer the crabs to a serving platter. Crack the claws and legs with nutcrackers or claw crackers and serve with the seasoned butter.

VARIATION 1 **STEAMED CRAB:** You can steam any fresh crab that is available in your area: stone crab claws, king crab legs, snow crab, and even the smaller blue crabs!

VARIATION 2 **INFUSED CRAB AND BUTTER:** Play with infusing the steaming liquid with 1 tablespoon of pickling spice or fresh herbs like dill and parsley. You can also change up the butter with a simple sprinkle of chopped chiles or a few pinches of truffle salt.

CRAB RANGOON

These deep-fried crab dumplings first hit the scene in 1956 at Trader Vic's, a popular Polynesian-style restaurant in San Francisco. The restaurant is closed, but these appetizers still exist in nearly every Asian restaurant across America, even though they aren't available in any Asian country. But who cares? They are delicious! **SERVES 4, AS AN APPETIZER**

PREP TIME: 20 minutes
COOK TIME: 15 minutes

4 ounces cream cheese, softened

4 ounces fresh or canned crabmeat, cartilage removed, picked through, and squeezed of extra moisture

1 scallion, finely chopped (white and green parts)

2 garlic cloves, minced

½ teaspoon Worcestershire sauce

2 teaspoons kosher salt, divided

Freshly ground black pepper

1 large egg, beaten

12 fresh wonton wrappers

3 cups canola oil, for deep frying

1. In a small bowl, mix together the cream cheese, crabmeat, scallion, garlic, and Worcestershire sauce until just combined. Stir in 1 teaspoon of salt and season with pepper.

2. Re-beat the egg. On a clean work surface, place a wonton wrapper. With your fingertip or a pastry brush, lightly brush the edges of the wrapper with the egg wash.

3. Place 1 teaspoon of crab filling in the middle of the wrapper. Fold the wrapper up by bringing the opposite corners together and lining the edges up together, sealing the seams to make an "X." Repeat the process with the remaining wonton wrappers and filling.

4. In a Dutch oven, heat the oil over medium heat to 375°F, or when the end of a wooden spoon dipped into the oil causes bubbling and sizzling.

5. Working in batches, place 3 or 4 rangoon in the hot oil and cook until brown and crispy, 4 to 5 minutes. Using a wire skimmer, transfer the rangoon to a wire rack to drain.

6. Lightly season the rangoon with salt. Serve immediately.

VARIATION 1 CURRIED CRAB RANGOON: Add 2 teaspoons of curry powder to the filling for curried crab rangoon.

VARIATION 2 BAKED CRAB RANGOON: If you would prefer not to deep fry, brush the dumplings with some melted butter and bake for 15 minutes in a 425°F oven.

CRAB AND CORN CHOWDER

This richly satisfying soup is a riff on New England clam chowder, using sweet corn and delicate crabmeat instead of clams. A personal note: I was born and raised in New York, which makes me a Manhattan clam chowder loyalist. If I am to make a white chowder, it will be corn and crab because clams would be treason. **SERVES 4**

PREP TIME: 15 minutes
COOK TIME: 30 minutes

2 tablespoons
unsalted butter

1 small yellow onion, cut
into ¼-inch dice

Kosher salt

Freshly ground
black pepper

2 tablespoons
all-purpose flour

Pinch cayenne pepper

4 cups whole milk

¼ cup heavy cream

¼ cup low-sodium fish
stock or clam juice

1 large Yukon gold potato,
peeled and cut into
¼-inch dice

2 cups frozen yellow corn
kernels, thawed

8 ounces lump crabmeat,
picked through

1 tablespoon fresh chives,
thinly sliced, for garnish

1. In a medium pot or Dutch oven over medium heat, melt the butter. Add the onion and a pinch of salt and pepper. Sauté for 4 minutes, or until the onion is soft and translucent.

2. Sprinkle the flour and cayenne over the onion and sauté until the flour has created a film in the bottom of the pot, 2 to 3 minutes.

3. Gradually add the milk, ½ cup at a time, stirring constantly to keep the flour from creating lumps. If the milk begins to thicken, turn the heat to medium-low. Stir in the fish stock and cream. The soup should begin to thicken.

4. Reduce the heat to low. Add the potatoes and corn and simmer, stirring occasionally, for about 12 minutes, until the potatoes are tender. Add the crabmeat and season with salt and pepper, and simmer for a few more minutes.

5. Divide the soup among bowls and garnish with the chives. Serve immediately.

VARIATION 1 **NEW ENGLAND CLAM CHOWDER:** To make this into New England clam chowder. Add 2 cups of chopped clams. I would also suggest sautéing a stalk of chopped celery with the onion.

VARIATION 2 **ROASTED CRAB AND CORN SOUP:** Make this soup next-level delicious. Roast corn on the cob and crab. Save the cobs and shells for the soup's stock.

CRAB HUSHPUPPIES

These light, fluffy fritters go upscale with the addition of crabmeat. The batter should be made while the oil is heating up. Since the batter will be deep fried as soon as the oil is at the right temperature, opening a can of crabmeat is the best option, since it's ready to go.

SERVES 4, AS A SIDE DISH OR APPETIZER

PREP TIME: 10 minutes
COOK TIME: 15 minutes

4 cups vegetable oil, for frying

1 cup cornmeal (preferably stone-ground)

¾ cup all-purpose flour

1 teaspoon baking powder

¼ teaspoon cayenne pepper

Kosher salt

Freshly ground black pepper

1 cup plus 2 tablespoons buttermilk

8 ounces lump crabmeat, picked over and blotted dry

2 large eggs, beaten

1 garlic clove, minced

2 scallions, finely chopped (white and green parts)

1. In a Dutch oven, heat the oil over medium-high heat to 375°F, or when the end of a wooden spoon dipped into the oil causes bubbling and sizzling. Set a wire rack over a baking sheet and set aside.

2. While the oil is heating, in a medium bowl, whisk together the cornmeal, flour, baking powder, and cayenne. Season with salt and pepper.

3. In another bowl, stir together the buttermilk, crabmeat, eggs, garlic, and scallions. Fold the buttermilk mixture into the flour mixture until just incorporated.

4. Working in batches, scoop rounded tablespoonfuls of the batter and, using a second spoon, gently nudge the batter off the spoon into the oil. Using a slotted spoon or wire skimmer, turn the hush puppies and fry until golden brown, about 3 minutes.

5. Transfer to the wire rack and lightly season with salt while still hot. Transfer to a platter and serve.

VARIATION 1 SHRIMP OR CATFISH HUSHPUPPIES: Chopped shrimp or flaked catfish make great substitutes.

VARIATION 2 SWEET AND SPICY HUSHPUPPIES: Add 1 tablespoon of minced fresh jalapeño to the batter to make it a sweet and spicy hushpuppy.

CRAB AND ARTICHOKE DIP

Every year, someone in my family makes this dish for our holiday gathering as an appetizer. We serve the dip with loads of crusty baguette slices. We always make the same mistake—not eating all day and then devouring this dip with all the bread, leaving no room for the actual meal. Every. Year. But this dip is so tasty and warm, I think secretly we actually look forward to ruining our dinner. **SERVES 4, AS AN APPETIZER**

PREP TIME: 10 minutes
COOK TIME: 30 minutes

1 (8-ounce) cream cheese package, at room temperature

1 cup mayonnaise

1 cup grated Monterey Jack cheese, divided

½ cup shredded Parmesan cheese

1 tablespoon Worcestershire sauce

2 dashes hot sauce (such as Tabasco)

Kosher salt

Freshly ground black pepper

1 pound lump crabmeat, picked through

1 (14-ounce) can artichoke hearts, drained and chopped

2 large garlic cloves, minced

3 scallions, thinly sliced (white and green parts)

2 tablespoons chopped fresh flat-leaf parsley, for garnish

1. Preheat the oven to 425°F.

2. In a large bowl, stir together the cream cheese, mayonnaise, ¾ cup of Monterey Jack, the Parmesan, Worcestershire sauce, and hot sauce. Season with salt and pepper.

3. Use the back of a wooden spoon to beat and soften the cream cheese mixture. It's okay if you still have some lumps. Stir in the crabmeat, artichoke hearts, garlic, and scallions until thoroughly combined.

4. Transfer the mixture to a 10-inch cast iron skillet or casserole dish and sprinkle with the remaining ¼ cup of Monterey Jack. Bake until golden and bubbly, 15 to 20 minutes.

5. Remove from the oven and garnish with the parsley. Allow the dip to cool for 10 minutes before serving.

VARIATION 1 CRAB, OLIVE, AND PIMENTO DIP: Use a 4-ounce jar of diced pimentos and ¼ cup of sliced olives or canned jalapeños instead of the artichokes.

VARIATION 2 MINI CRAB MELTS: Instead of making it into a dip, spread the mixture on sliced baguette and broil to make little crab melt appetizers.

CHEESY CRAB STRUDEL

This pastry's beautiful braid looks and sounds complicated, but it's actually made with a simple technique of overlapping strips of pastry. It makes a terrific appetizer; however, if you serve this alongside a vinegary green salad, it makes an elegant lunch. **SERVES 4 TO 8, AS AN APPETIZER**

PREP TIME: 20 minutes
COOK TIME: 45 minutes, plus 30 minutes to cool

3 tablespoons extra-virgin olive oil

1 medium white onion, cut into ¼-inch dice

4 garlic cloves, minced

Kosher salt

Freshly ground black pepper

1½ cups frozen yellow corn, thawed

1 (4-ounce) jar diced pimentos, drained

1 teaspoon ground cumin

1 teaspoon smoked paprika

1 pound lump crabmeat, picked though

1½ cups shredded Monterey Jack cheese

½ cup minced fresh cilantro leaves

All-purpose flour, for dusting

2 sheets frozen puff pastry, thawed

1 large egg, beaten

1. Preheat the oven to 400°F. Line two baking sheets with aluminum foil or parchment paper and set aside.

2. In a nonstick skillet, heat the olive oil over medium-high heat. When shimmery wavy lines run through the oil, add the onion and garlic and sauté until the onion is soft and translucent, about 7 minutes. Season with salt and pepper.

3. Add the corn, pimentos, cumin, and paprika and sauté for another 2 minutes. Transfer to a bowl and fold in the crabmeat, Monterey Jack, and cilantro. Set aside to cool slightly.

4. Lightly dust a clean work surface with flour. Unfold one sheet of puff pastry. Using a floured rolling pin, roll the dough out slightly into a 16-by-12-inch rectangle. Transfer the pastry to the prepared baking sheet.

5. Position the pan with the shortest side facing you. Spoon half the crab mixture lengthwise down the center of the pastry. Cut horizontal strips, 2 inches apart, along the long sides of the pastry, leaving ½ inch of space around the filling. ❯

6. Starting at one end, fold the pastry strips over the filling, alternating sides each time, to cover the filling and make a braided effect. Repeat the process with the remaining pastry sheet and crabmeat mixture. Brush the pastries with the beaten egg.

7. Bake for 35 minutes or until the pastries are golden brown. Let the pastries cool on the baking sheet on a wire rack for 30 minutes before serving.

8. To serve, transfer the pastries to platters and slice each pastry into 4 (3-inch-wide) pieces. Serve warm.

VARIATION 1 CRAB AND ARTICHOKE STRUDEL: The Crab and Artichoke Dip (see page 142) is also a lovely and rich filling for this pastry.

VARIATION 2 SALMON OR SHRIMP STRUDEL: Substitute flaked salmon or chopped cooked shrimp in the filling. It's really versatile and can go with anything.

CIOPPINO

Cioppino, a flavorful tomato-based stew, is another recipe that originates from San Francisco. Dungeness crab is usually used, but any type of crab that is available wherever you are will work perfectly here. **SERVES 4**

PREP TIME: 15 minutes
COOK TIME: 30 minutes

2 tablespoons extra-virgin olive oil

Pinch red pepper flakes

2 garlic cloves, thinly sliced

1 small yellow onion, cut into ¼-inch dice

Kosher salt

Freshly ground black pepper

1 (14-ounce) can crushed tomatoes, with their juices

2 cups low-sodium fish or shellfish stock

1 (2-pound) scrubbed Dungeness crab, cleaned and quartered

16 clams, cleaned

16 mussels, cleaned

12 large shrimp (U31/40), peeled and deveined

1 (4-ounce) salmon fillet, cut into 2-inch pieces

4 ounces Bay scallops

2 tablespoons minced fresh flat-leaf parsley, for garnish

Garlic bread, for serving

1. In a Dutch oven, heat the olive oil and red pepper flakes over medium heat. When shimmery wavy lines run through the oil, add the garlic and onion, cover the pot, and sweat the onion for about 4 minutes, stirring occasionally.

2. Season with salt and pepper and continue to cook, uncovered, until the liquid has evaporated, another 2 minutes.

3. Add the tomatoes and sauté for 3 minutes. Add the fish stock, increase the heat to medium-high, and bring to a boil. Lower the heat to medium-low and simmer for 10 minutes, until the liquid reduces slightly and the flavors concentrate.

4. Add the crab, clams, mussels, shrimp, salmon, and scallops. Season with salt and pepper and gently fold to combine. Cover and cook for 8 to 10 minutes, or until all the seafood is cooked.

5. To serve, divide the stew among soup bowls and garnish with the parsley. Serve hot with lots of garlic bread.

VARIATION 1 CIOPPINO WITH A TWIST: Use any seafood you like. Calamari, cod, and sea scallops are all good substitutes, but whatever is available and fresh at the market will work. As long as you have a combination of flaky fish, shellfish, and mollusks, cioppino can contain anything.

VARIATION 2 HEARTY CIOPPINO STEW: Make a heartier stew by adding some diced potatoes or spooning the stew over cooked pasta shells.

Clams Casino, page 149

CHAPTER 10

CLAMS AND MUSSELS

There are three types of mussels available: Mediterranean, blue, and green-lipped. Mediterranean mussels are large and plump. Blue mussels offer a more intense flavor. Green-lipped have a bright orange flesh. Farm-raised blue mussels, known as PEI, are the most widely available. They originate from Prince Edward Island, Canada.

Clams can be broken down into two major categories: hard shell and soft shell. From the smallest to largest, they include Manila, littleneck, cherry-stones, chowder, and quahogs. The smaller ones are tender and sweeter, while the larger ones are tough and should be chopped up before adding to a recipe. Soft-shell clams are available in different forms: steamers, known as Ipswich; long narrow clams called razor clams; and the phallic looking geoduck clam (pronounced gooey-duck).

You can get clams and mussels from the market fresh, frozen, or canned. Fresh clams and mussels should be firmly closed and feel heavy. Be sure to tap on any clams with an opened shell. If it remains open, they've expired.

Take home live shellfish in an open bag so they can breathe. Scrub them clean under cold water, and for mussels, pull off the stringy material, also known as their beards. Farm-raised mussels are usually debearded for the consumer.

Store the shellfish for up to 24 hours in a refrigerator in a colander, set in bowl to catch any water, and drape them with a wet paper towel to keep them hydrated. After cooking discard those that remain closed.

STEAMED MUSSELS IN WHITE WINE

You don't need much time, money, effort, kitchen equipment, or skill to make this amazingly simple and classic dish. Last year, my husband and I stayed in a hotel room with a kitchenette with my parents. After days and days eating in restaurants, we were craving a home-cooked meal. I found a local market and knocked this together with some bread, cheese, and wine, and we had a lovely meal in our room. Mom and Dad still say this was best meal they had on the entire trip. **SERVES 4**

PREP TIME: 20 minutes
COOK TIME: 15 minutes

4 tablespoons (½ stick) unsalted butter

2 small shallots, finely chopped

6 large garlic cloves, thinly sliced

Kosher salt

Pinch freshly ground black pepper

½ cup dry white wine (such as Sauvignon blanc)

4 pounds mussels, cleaned and debearded

¼ cup coarsely chopped fresh flat-leaf parsley

Crusty bread, for serving

1. In a large Dutch oven over medium-low heat, melt the butter. Add the shallots and garlic and season with salt and pepper. Sauté until the shallots and garlic wilt, 2 to 3 minutes. Do not let them take on any color.

2. Add the wine and bring to a boil. Add the mussels and stir them a few times in the wine. Lower the heat to medium-low and cook for 5 to 7 minutes, or until the mussels open, lifting the lid halfway through cooking to give them a stir.

3. Remove from heat and remove any mussels that have not opened. Toss in the parsley. Serve the mussels with crusty bread.

VARIATION 1 STEAMED MUSSELS AND FRIES: If you serve these with a side of French fries, then you've made moules-frites! My friend Ken loves them with a side of homemade aioli. For homemade fries, follow chapter 5's recipe for Classic Fish and Chips (see page 76). And make the Saffron Aioli from this chapter (see page 152).

VARIATION 2 THAI-INFUSED STEAMED MUSSELS: One of my favorite variations is a Thai-infused dish with lemongrass, lime juice, and coconut milk added to the shallots and garlic. Add ½ cup of light coconut milk and 1 large lemongrass stalk that has been peeled and minced. Add the lime juice at the very end, stirring just before serving.

CLAMS CASINO

My Dad loves clams casino. Actually, I think he just loves to say the words. It certainly has more cachet than "clams on the half-shell." Though it originated in Rhode Island, you can find it on nearly every menu in New York's Little Italy. **SERVES 4, AS AN APPETIZER**

PREP TIME: 20 minutes
COOK TIME: 30 minutes

12 littleneck clams, scrubbed well under cold water

¼ cup water

4 bacon slices, cut crosswise into ¼-inch strips

1 tablespoon unsalted butter

1 (4-ounce) jar diced pimentos, drained

1 small shallot, finely chopped

2 garlic cloves, minced

Kosher salt

Freshly ground black pepper

¾ cup panko bread crumbs

2 tablespoons minced fresh flat-leaf parsley

1 tablespoon grated Parmesan cheese

1 lemon, cut into wedges, for serving

1. In a medium saucepan over medium-high heat, combine the clams and water. Cover and steam the clams for 6 to 7 minutes, or until they have completely opened. Remove from the heat and set aside to cool slightly.

2. When the clams are cool enough to handle, remove the top shells (the deeper shell is the bottom), run a spoon under the clam to dislodge it from the shell, and turn it over. In a 9-by-13-inch baking dish, arrange the clams in their half shells. Strain the clam juice from the pot and reserve.

3. In a nonstick pan over medium-high heat, cook the bacon slices until just brown but not yet crisp. Using a slotted spoon, transfer to a plate lined with paper towels and set aside. Pour off the bacon fat and discard, but don't discard any brown bits from the bacon.

4. Return the pan to medium-high heat and add the butter. When the butter has melted, add the pimentos, shallot, and garlic and sauté until soft, about 4 minutes. Lightly season with salt and pepper. >

5. Add 2 tablespoons of reserved clam juice and deglaze the pan. Continue cooking until the clam juice has evaporated, about 2 minutes. Remove from the heat and set the pan aside to cool for a few minutes.

6. Preheat the broiler.

7. In the slightly cooled pan, stir together the bread crumbs, parsley, and Parmesan and divide the bread crumb mixture between the clams. Top with the bacon slices.

8. Broil for 3 to 5 minutes, or until the bacon is crispy and the bread crumbs are toasty brown. Serve garnished with lemon wedges.

VARIATION 1 MOULES GRATINÉES: Meaning "baked mussels" in French, this dish uses mussels instead of clams. Mussels are much smaller than clams, so be sure to prepare twice as many mussels and cook them for half the time.

VARIATION 2 SMOKY STUFFED CLAMS: For a smokier flavor, add 1 teaspoon of smoked paprika to the bread crumbs mixture and use diced Spanish chorizo instead of bacon.

LINGUINE ALLE VONGOLE

My absolute hands-down favorite dish: linguine with clams. This simple pasta dish can be made for a late-night meal or an absolute stunner of a date-night dinner. Either way, it's one of those perfect recipes that belongs in your repertoire. For a fresh twist, we added cilantro, but that's not traditional. **SERVES 4**

PREP TIME: 10 minutes
COOK TIME: 25 minutes

12 ounces linguine
or spaghetti

3 tablespoons extra-virgin
olive oil

1 small yellow onion, cut
into ¼-inch dice

Pinch of kosher salt

4 garlic cloves, thinly sliced

Generous pinch red
pepper flakes

3 pounds littleneck
clams, scrubbed and
picked through

½ cup dry white wine (such
as Sauvignon blanc)

3 tablespoons
unsalted butter

2 tablespoons coarsely
chopped fresh
flat-leaf parsley

2 tablespoons coarsely
chopped fresh cilantro

Juice of ½ lemon

1. In a large stockpot of boiling water, cook the linguini according to package instructions, about 10 minutes. Drain the pasta, reserving 1 cup of pasta water.

2. While the water comes to a boil, in a large sauté pan, skillet, over medium-high heat, heat the oil. Add the onion and salt and sauté until the onion is translucent, about 4 minutes. Add the garlic and the red pepper flakes and sauté for a few seconds more, or until the garlic is fragrant.

3. Toss in the clams and wine and cover. Steam for 8 to 10 minutes, until the majority of the clams have opened. Discard any that are still closed and add the butter, parsley, and cilantro.

4. Toss the pasta in the pan with the clams. Add the lemon juice. If the sauce looks a little dry, add a small amount of the pasta water. Serve immediately.

VARIATION 1 SIMPLE WEEKNIGHT CLAM LINGUINI: No fresh clams? No problem! One (14.5-ounce) can of clams will do. Add the whole can, juice and all.

VARIATION 2 FRUTTI DI MARE: Use 1 pound each of clams, mussels, and shrimp and 1 cup of lump crabmeat. Cook the clams first, add the mussels and shrimp halfway through, and then add the crabmeat at the end.

BROILED MUSSELS WITH FENNEL AND SAFFRON AIOLI

The broiler is a very underrated and underused feature in the oven. Often you can flash-broil food and achieve a super-hot, browned, and crispy surface in just a matter of moments. Since mussels have such thin shells, they cook in a short amount of time. Since there is very little fat being cooked with the mussels and vegetables, adding dollops of a fragrant saffron aioli helps create a rich sauce that you can soak up with lots of crusty bread. **SERVES 4**

PREP TIME: 15 minutes
COOK TIME: 10 minutes

FOR THE AIOLI

Generous pinch saffron threads

1 tablespoon hot water

1 large egg yolk

2 teaspoons freshly squeezed lemon juice

Kosher salt

Pinch freshly ground black pepper

½ cup vegetable oil

½ cup extra-virgin olive oil

1 garlic clove, minced to a fine paste with a pinch of salt ❯

1. To make the aioli, in a small bowl, steep the saffron in the water until it's bright orange.

2. In a blender, combine the egg yolk and lemon juice. Season with salt and pepper and mix until combined.

3. With the blender running, very slowly drizzle in the oil, just a few drops at a time to start. As the aioli begins to thicken, the oil can be poured a little faster in a thin steady stream. If the mixture becomes too thick, add a little more lemon juice or water and continue to mix until the oil is incorporated.

4. Add the garlic paste and saffron water and blend. Transfer to a bowl, cover with plastic wrap, and refrigerate until ready to use.

5. Preheat the broiler. Line a baking sheet with aluminum foil.

6. To make the mussels, on the prepared baking sheet, toss the fennel, leeks, and olive oil. Season with salt and pepper. Broil for 3 to 4 minutes, or until the vegetables are soft. Remove the pan from the broiler.

FOR THE MUSSELS

2 large fennel bulbs, each trimmed and cut into 8 wedges, fronds reserved for garnish

1 large leek, trimmed, cleaned, and thinly sliced

2 tablespoons extra-virgin olive oil

Kosher salt

Freshly ground black pepper

4 pounds fresh mussels, picked through

Crusty baguette, sliced, for serving

7. Add the mussels in a single layer to the pan and return to the broiler. Broil for 3 to 4 minutes, or until the mussels open.

8. Discard any mussels that are still closed and transfer the open mussels and vegetables to a warm shallow serving bowl. Add dollops of aioli on top, garnishing with the fennel fronds. Serve immediately with lots of crusty baguette slices.

VARIATION 1 BROILED SHRIMP AND FISH: Broiled shrimp and chunks of salmon or tuna would work well in this preparation style. Add other vegetables such as asparagus, zucchini, or artichokes—virtually any vegetable would go well with this aioli!

VARIATION 2 BROILED MUSSEL SANDWICH: Layer the broiled vegetables, seafood, and aioli in a crusty French roll for a satisfying sandwich.

FRIED CLAMS

Fried clams are a New England delicacy. I was perhaps seven years old the first time I had them. My dad took us to a tiny crowded seafood shack on Cape Cod, and we snacked on baskets of freshly fried clams all afternoon. Over the years, I've tried to recreate that texture. The key is making sure the oil is so hot that the outside batter fries up crunchy by the time the interior of the clam cooks through. **SERVES 4, AS AN APPETIZER**

PREP TIME: 15 minutes
COOK TIME: 20 minutes

2 pounds littleneck or steamer clams, scrubbed, cleaned, and picked through, or 2 (8-ounce) cans clams, drained

¼ cup water

1½ cups buttermilk

1 cup corn flour

1 cup all-purpose flour

½ teaspoon baking powder

2 teaspoons Old Bay Seasoning

Kosher salt

Freshly ground black pepper

Vegetable oil, for deep frying

1 lemon, cut into wedges, for serving

1. Set a wire rack over a baking sheet and set aside.

2. In a large saucepan over high heat, combine the clams and water. Steam the clams until they open, 5 to 8 minutes. Transfer to a bowl and discard any clams that have not opened. Set aside for a few minutes to cool.

3. When the clams are cool enough to handle, using a spoon, scrape each clam off its bottom shell and transfer to a small bowl. Pour the buttermilk over the clams and stir to coat.

4. In a separate bowl, stir together the corn flour, all-purpose flour, baking powder, and Old Bay seasoning. Season with salt and pepper.

5. In a Dutch oven or large saucepan over medium-high heat, heat 3 inches of vegetable oil to 375°F, or when the end of a wooden spoon dipped into the oil causes bubbling and sizzling.

6. Working in batches and using a slotted spoon, carefully lift about one-third of the clams from the buttermilk, shaking gently to allow excess buttermilk to drip back into the bowl.

7. Transfer the clams to the flour mixture and gently toss to coat. Remove the clams and shake off excess flour.

8. Using a wire skimmer, lower the clams into the oil and push them around so they don't stick together in a clump. Fry for 2 to 3 minutes, moving them occasionally but gently so they cook evenly, until they are golden brown and crispy.

9. Transfer the fried clams to the wire rack to drain. Lightly season with salt.

10. Transfer the fried clams to a platter and serve hot with the lemon on the side.

VARIATION 1 FRIED SHRIMP AND MUSSELS: Frozen shrimp and mussels fry up beautifully. As soon as they thaw, blot them dry with paper towels before adding to the buttermilk. For a spicier kick, add a dash of Tabasco sauce or sriracha to the buttermilk.

VARIATION 2 BEER-BATTERED CLAMS: You can make beer-battered clams by substituting half the amount of buttermilk for beer. A light pale ale works better than something heavy.

MANHATTAN CLAM CHOWDER

I'll admit it: I am partial to red clam chowder (as we called it in New York) over white clam chowder. I find the zesty tomato-based soup more flavorful than the creamier white soup (and, okay, growing up I struggled with lactose intolerance). There isn't a feud more famous than red versus white clam chowder, except for maybe the feud between the Hatfields and the McCoys. **SERVES 4 TO 6**

PREP TIME: 15 minutes
COOK TIME: 55 minutes

4 cups water

24 to 36 medium cherrystone or littleneck clams, scrubbed clean and picked through

2 bay leaves

4 ounces bacon, diced

1 yellow onion, cut into ¼-inch dice

2 celery stalks, cut into ¼-inch dice

2 carrots, peeled and cut into ¼-inch dice

2 garlic cloves, minced

Pinch red pepper flakes

Kosher salt

Freshly ground black pepper

1 (28-ounce) can diced tomatoes, with their juices

2 large russet potatoes, peeled and cut into ½-inch cubes

1. In a Dutch oven, heat the water over medium-high heat. Add the clams and the bay leaves and bring to a boil. Lower the heat to medium, cover, and simmer for 12 to 15 minutes, or until the clams have opened.

2. Using a wire skimmer, transfer the clams to a bowl, discard any that haven't opened, and set aside to cool.

3. Strain the clam broth through a sieve lined with cheesecloth and set aside. When the clams are cool enough to handle, using a spoon, scrape the clams from their shells and transfer to a small bowl.

4. Rinse the pot and place over medium-high heat. Add the bacon and cook for 5 to 7 minutes, or until it's crisp. Using a slotted spoon, transfer the bacon to the clam bowl, leaving the bacon fat in the pan.

5. Add the onion, celery, and carrots and sauté until the vegetables are soft and the onion is translucent, 8 to 9 minutes. Add the garlic and red pepper flakes and sauté until the garlic is fragrant, about 1 minute. Season with salt and pepper.

6. Add the tomatoes and cook for 2 minutes. Season with salt and pepper. Add the potatoes and 4 cups of reserved clam broth. Raise the heat to high, bring the soup to a boil, then lower the heat back down to medium-low. Simmer for 15 minutes, or until the potatoes are soft.

7. Stir in the clams and bacon and simmer for 5 minutes, or until the clams are heated through.

8. To serve, ladle the soup into soup bowls. Serve hot.

VARIATION 1 CREAMY MANHATTAN CLAM CHOWDER: You can thicken this soup slightly by stirring in a beurre manie into the soup before serving. Make a paste with 1 tablespoon each of unsalted butter and all-purpose flour and stir that into the soup as it is simmering. As the butter melts, it distributes the starch granules, which will gelatinize and thicken the soup slightly.

VARIATION 2 MUSSEL CHOWDER: Forget about calling this Manhattan Clam Chowder and use mussels instead. It's delicious!

WHITE CLAM PIZZA

Frank Pepe Pizzeria in New Haven, Connecticut, one of the oldest and most famous pizzerias in America, is home to their signature white clam pizza. Its simplicity is what makes it so amazing—no sauce, just clams, some garlic, some herbs, and a little bit of cheese (never ever mozzarella). This isn't exactly the same recipe, but it's pretty close. If you buy store-made dough, this pizza makes a terrific weeknight dinner, given its simplicity. **SERVES 4 TO 6**

PREP TIME: 20 minutes, plus 2 hours to rise
COOK TIME: 15 minutes

FOR THE PIZZA DOUGH

1 cup lukewarm water

1 teaspoon active dry yeast (¼ ounce)

½ teaspoon sugar

1 cup all-purpose flour

3 tablespoons extra-virgin olive oil, divided

2 teaspoons kosher salt ❭

1. To make the pizza dough, in a small bowl, combine the water, yeast, and sugar. Let sit for 10 minutes, or until it begins to foam.

2. In a large bowl, using a wooden spoon, stir together the flour, yeast mixture, 2 tablespoons of oil, and the salt until a dough comes together. Turn the dough out onto a clean work surface and knead with your hands until it is smooth and elastic, 5 to 10 minutes.

3. Drizzle the remaining 1 tablespoon of oil into the bowl and spread it around the inside. Place the dough in the bowl and flip to coat in oil. Cover the bowl with plastic wrap and keep it in a warm spot until doubled in size, about 2 hours.

4. Preheat the oven to 500°F. If you have a pizza stone, set it on the lowest rack of your oven.

5. To make the pizza, on a lightly floured surface, roll the dough to a 10-inch circle about ¼ inch thick.

FOR THE PIZZA

All-purpose flour,
for dusting

2 tablespoons semolina
flour, for dusting

½ cup shredded
low-moisture
mozzarella cheese

¼ cup grated Pecorino
Romano cheese

1 (8-ounce) can whole or
chopped clams, drained

3 garlic cloves, minced

1 tablespoon coarsely
chopped fresh
oregano leaves

2 tablespoons extra-virgin
olive oil

6. Dust a pizza peel (if using the stone) or a baking sheet with the semolina flour and slide the dough onto it. Sprinkle evenly with the mozzarella, Pecorino, clams, garlic, and oregano. Drizzle with olive oil and transfer the pizza to the oven, either to the stone or on the baking sheet.

7. Bake until golden brown and bubbling, 10 to 12 minutes. Let the pizza rest for a few minutes before slicing.

VARIATION 1   WHITE SHRIMP PIZZA: Shrimp pizza is a wonderful thing. Try using tiny shrimp or chopped larger shrimp as a topping. Don't use precooked shrimp. It will be tough and overcooked by the time the pizza is ready.

VARIATION 2   CLAMS AND PANCETTA PIZZA: Add some cooked pancetta or bacon as an additional pizza topping with the clams. It's very tasty!

CHORIZO AND CLAMS

A sauté pan or skillet that is wide and shallow with straight walls is perfect for making this recipe. If you are the type to sip wine while you cook, adding a splash of whatever you are enjoying to the pan works great. Or beer. Beer works, too. Make sure you have lots of crusty bread to eat with this dish! **SERVES 4**

PREP TIME: 15 minutes
COOK TIME: 25 minutes

2 tablespoons extra-virgin olive oil

1 small yellow onion, cut into ½-inch cubes

3 garlic cloves, thinly sliced

Kosher salt

Freshly ground black pepper

1 Spanish chorizo sausage, casing removed and cut into ½-inch chunks

2 teaspoons smoked paprika

2 Roma tomatoes, coarsely chopped

36 littleneck or cherrystone clams, scrubbed clean and picked over

½ cup dry white wine (such as Sauvignon blanc)

½ cup coarsely chopped fresh flat-leaf parsley

1. Heat a large shallow sauté pan or skillet over medium heat and add the olive oil, onion, and garlic. Season with salt and pepper and cover for 10 minutes to sweat the onion.

2. Uncover and add the chorizo and paprika. Sauté for 3 to 4 minutes, until the fat begins to render out of the sausage. Add the tomatoes and continue to sauté for another 2 minutes.

3. Add the clams and wine and cover the pan. Steam for 8 to 10 minutes, or until the clams have completely opened. Discard any clams that do not open. Remove from the heat and toss with the parsley.

4. Evenly divide among shallow bowls and serve immediately.

VARIATION 1 CHORIZO AND MUSSELS: You can add mussels to this dish, but add them during the last 5 minutes of cooking. Mussel shells are thinner than clam shells and do not take as long to cook. If you add them at the same time as the clams, they will be overcooked by the time the clams are ready.

VARIATION 2 FENNEL, CLAM, AND CHORIZO SPAGHETTI: This is delicious served over cooked spaghetti noodles or even served with roasted potatoes. To add more vegetables, try chopped fennel or sliced celery. The extra crunchy texture is amazing.

MEASUREMENT CONVERSIONS

VOLUME EQUIVALENTS (LIQUID)

STANDARD	US STANDARD (OUNCES)	METRIC (APPROXIMATE)
2 tablespoons	1 fl. oz.	30 mL
¼ cup	2 fl. oz.	60 mL
½ cup	4 fl. oz.	120 mL
1 cup	8 fl. oz.	240 mL
1½ cups	12 fl. oz.	355 mL
2 cups or 1 pint	16 fl. oz.	475 mL
4 cups or 1 quart	32 fl. oz.	1 L
1 gallon	128 fl. oz.	4 L

OVEN TEMPERATURES

FAHRENHEIT (F)	CELSIUS (C) (APPROXIMATE)
250°	120°
300°	150°
325°	165°
350°	180°
375°	190°
400°	200°
425°	220°
450°	230°

VOLUME EQUIVALENTS (DRY)

STANDARD	METRIC (APPROXIMATE)
⅛ teaspoon	0.5 mL
¼ teaspoon	1 mL
½ teaspoon	2 mL
¾ teaspoon	4 mL
1 teaspoon	5 mL
1 tablespoon	15 mL
¼ cup	59 mL
⅓ cup	79 mL
½ cup	118 mL
⅔ cup	156 mL
¾ cup	177 mL
1 cup	235 mL
2 cups or 1 pint	475 mL
3 cups	700 mL
4 cups or 1 quart	1 L

WEIGHT EQUIVALENTS

STANDARD	METRIC (APPROXIMATE)
½ ounce	15 g
1 ounce	30 g
2 ounces	60 g
4 ounces	115 g
8 ounces	225 g
12 ounces	340 g
16 ounces or 1 pound	455 g

RESOURCES

Environmental Defense Fund (EDF). This is a nonprofit environmental advocacy group based in the United States. The group works on issues such as global warming, ecosystem restoration, oceans, and human health. (http://seafood.edf.org)

Marine Stewardship Council. This is a global nonprofit organization based in London, England. It sets the standards for sustainable fishing. Their website is a host of information for consumers to make sustainable choices when shopping for seafood. (https://www.msc.org)

Ocean Conservancy. This is a nonprofit environmental advocacy group based in Washington, DC, shaping policy that helps protect wildlife in the ocean. (https://oceanconservancy.org)

Seafood Watch. This program run by the Monterey Bay Aquarium is one of the best-known sites for consumers to look up information about sustainable seafood so they can make informed decisions on purchasing seafood or ordering in restaurants. (https://www.seafoodwatch.org)

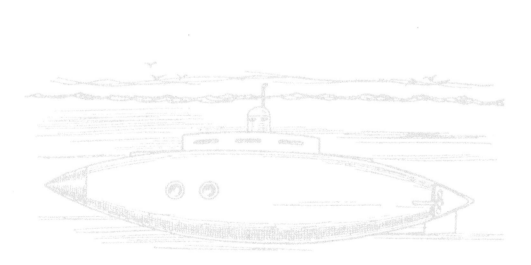

REFERENCES

The Cuisine of Southeast Asia and Vietnam

http://www.cafemeetingplace.com/pdf/lesson/lesson_dec07.pdf

Health Benefits of Eating Fish

https://www.healthline.com/nutrition/11-health-benefits-of-fish#section1

https://health.gov/dietaryguidelines/2015/

Mercury Poisoning: Health Effects

https://www.livescience.com/53837-mercury-poisoning.html

https://www.fda.gov/food/consumers/advice-about-eating-fish

Omega-3 Fatty Acids: Health Benefits

https://www.heart.org/en/healthy-living/healthy-eating/eat-smart/fats/fish
-and-omega-3-fatty-acids

https://www.ncbi.nlm.nih.gov/pubmed/16531187

https://health.usnews.com/wellness/slideshows/13-best-fish-high-in-omega
-3sand-environment-friendly

INDEX

ACKNOWLEDGMENTS

There are more people who deserve my thanks than I can list here. I am grateful to everyone who pitched in ideas and suggestions to include in this book. Messages from friends and family bearing encouragement during this process have lifted and carried me through the challenging moments, when words couldn't come from my brain through to the page. Special thanks to Renate Valencia for her recipe advice and technical assistance.

To Chef Mia Chambers, there are no appropriate words to convey my gratitude. Mia's passion, skills, and talents have been a huge influence on my career. Mia taught me nearly everything that I know now about effectively teaching a cooking class, writing recipes, and delivering everything we do with grace and warmth.

Thank you, with deepest gratitude to Elizabeth, Carolyn, Katherine, and the entire production team at Callisto Media for making this book possible. I couldn't believe my luck when Elizabeth reached out to discuss a cookbook project and for pairing me with my editors, Carolyn and Katherine, who have been so supportive, helpful, and patient.

I am indebted to my instructors at City College of San Francisco: Chef Ron Ng, Chef Keith Hammerich, Chef John Oakley, Chef Mark Hodgson, Chef Aaron Ogden, Chef Erwin Pirolt, Mr. Christopher Stellman, Ms. Tannis Reinhertz, Ms. Claire Muller-Moseley, and Chef Edward Hamilton, who not only gave me the foundational techniques and principles of culinary arts and hospitality but also encouraged me to become the best at whatever I wanted to do. They taught me respect for food and respect for others, and their daily interactions with others were examples for me to follow.

Thank you to my colleagues and partners from Sur La Table: Katy Martin, Alexis DePaolis, Stefanie Boettner, Donna Wolfe, Marc Favia, B. B. Huff, Steph Kuo, Mark Brewington, Liz Prado, Igor Breyman, Christy Wolf, Lynn Kunkel, Sean Halasz, Karla Silva, Tony Crane, Alex Le, Jennifer Johnson, Ben Rosenfeld, and all of my chef instructors and kitchen assistants. Their hard work and commitment to our customers has been my inspiration. Managing the cooking school is more like living in a community devoted to bringing joy to our custom-ers through cooking and food.

   To my family, I thank them most of all for always being there for me. Their unconditional love and support help me move forward every day. And thank you to my husband, Paul, for believing in me and letting me follow my dreams. I love you.

ABOUT THE AUTHOR

Terri Dien is native New Yorker living in the San Francisco Bay Area. In 2003, she left political consulting to pursue her lifelong passion and enrolled in City College of San Francisco's Culinary Arts and Hospitality Studies program. She worked in restaurants, in both savory and pastry roles, and has also taught cooking classes for nearly 15 years for Draeger's Cooking School, South San Francisco Parks and Recreation Department, and Sur La Table. She currently works as Executive Program Chef for Child Care at Google, providing delicious plant-forward meals for children and their educators. Terri lives in San Mateo, California, with her husband, Paul, and their cats, Rosie, Sarah, and Henry. Keep in touch by following @ChefTerriDien on Instagram!

CPSIA information can be obtained
at www.ICGtesting.com
Printed in the USA
JSHW051531100222
22651JS00002B/3